# Love, War, Fire, Wind

## Looking Out from North America's Skull

poems by
**Eliot Katz**

drawings by
**William T. Ayton**

# Acknowledgments

Thanks to the editors of the following journals, anthologies, and online publications in which some of this book's poems and prose pieces originally appeared: *100+ Poets Against the War, 101 Poemes Contre La Guerre, Arbella, Ars Poetica, The Battle of Seattle, Big Hammer, Big Scream, Boog City,* commondreams.org, counterpunch.org, *Home Planet News, Left Curve,* litkicks.com, *Logos: A Journal of Modern Society and Culture* (www.logosjournal.com), *Long Shot, The Louisiana Review, MindFire,* mobylives.com, *Napalm Health Spa, New York Nights, New York Quarterly, Paterson Literary Review, Poetry After 9/11: An Anthology of New York Poets,* poetsagainstthewar.org, *Rattapallax, Sanctuary, Van Gogh's Ear, Voices of Reason, Wildflowers, The World the Sixties Made.* Some of the poems in this collection, as well as some earlier poems and prose by Eliot Katz, may be found online on Jim Cohn's Museum of American Poetics website at www.poetspath.com/exhibits/eliotkatz. Many of the poems in the first and third sections of this collection were previously published in two 2007 chapbooks: *View from the Big Woods;* and *When the Skyline Crumbles: Poems for the Bush Years.*

For more information, please visit: www.narcissuspublications.com

ISBN: 978-0-578-00650-5

FIRST EDITION

# Love, War, Fire, Wind

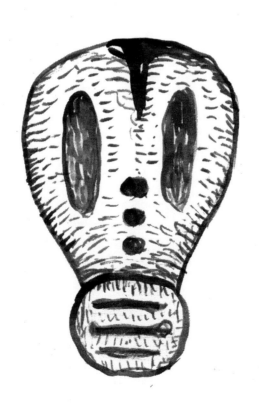

# Contents

### III. When the Skyline Crumbles: Poems for the Bush Years (2001-2007)

### Coda

# I. View from the Big Woods:
## Poems from North America's Skull

# Helicopter Ride

A low-flying helicopter through the Canadian drizzle
takes us 45 minutes over millions of acres of evergreen forest,
steep cliffs, streams, some oil rigs, some clear-cut land
       laid bare by mountain loggers.
The sight is breathtaking, a little scary—
if we crashed these forests, who would find us?

We're taking a helicopter because dirt roads
       are too soaked from rains to drive.
Vivian in back seat talks to Terry the pilot
about which direction best to approach Nose Mountain
       to avoid clouds.
Terry turns to me: "Do they have taxis like this in New York?"

2000

## These Beautiful Territories

The cloud outside the window is shaped like an angel
The gods have forgotten to say goodbye to these beautiful territories
It's impossible to keep shoes unmuddy along these trails
Danny was right, I should have brought a pair of hiking boots
Oprah's rituals for recently divorced find their way onto
           one of two channels in the mountain forest cabin
What's the trick to self-esteem, to mindfulness?
What's the trick to working one's way through all the damn tricks
           and getting to heart of the matter?
What's the heart matter in midst of a million poplar trees?
How wander muddy trails to right spirit, right action,
           end of grudges, compassion for all, the path
           to suffering's end?
I'm getting older—how wonderful it feels to find a new kind spirit
           as perhaps company for the next journey
One learns to release urban reliances here taking an aching back
           out to outhouse first thing in the morning
What history lessons are they teaching George Washboard Bush
           back in the States tonight?
Kerouac the Canadian said trees don't talk good
It's true! I can't tell what the hell they're saying!
Wooo taaacaaa waaaahhhhh eeeeeeeeee
But for some reason they cuddle up like longtime friends.
I give them advice—Duck the buzzsaw! Slip the lightning!
Hold your nose when the trucks drive by!
These trees will outlast America's next president
           whether it's Slicker or Dumber
& love will arrive with new water buckets to quench our thirst

2000

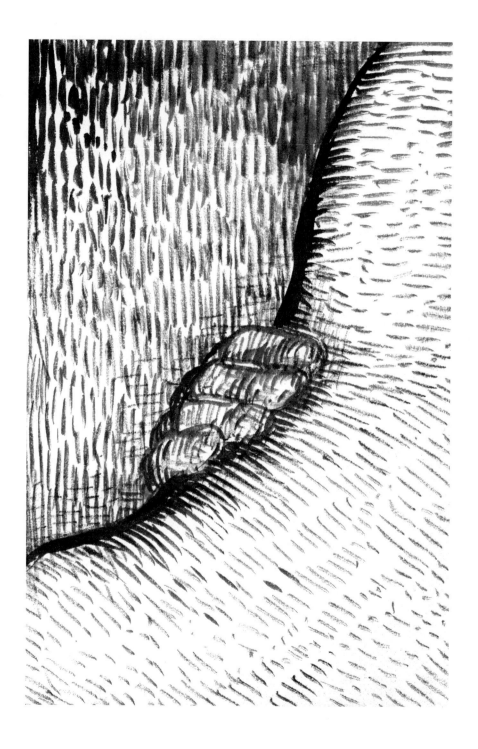

# 7 Types of Bliss

*—for Vivian*

No fires on the forest horizon but beautiful blue smoke emanating from
      inside.
Vibrations at perfect complementary pitch from subatomic strings behind
      eyelids to moans and screams echoing across the pine tops.
7 hands, 49 positions, 2401 ecstasies, infinite beauty & kind clear light
      with generator on or off.
I thought a bumblebee in flowers near the porch sounded like a moose
      calling from distant woods, we're a long way from Manhattan.
Smooth strides calm intelligence going about cabin firetower tasks,
      full bookcases, those eyes, that body, those hands, that love.
Rock & rolling across the galaxy like next week we'll be 3,000 miles apart,
      like neutrinos shot from the sun that will stop for nothing and no
      one.
Like nothing, like emptiness, like total joyous effort, like no thing known
      or unknown, like the orgasmic energy of the universe is present
      in every touch or stroke if only the air is clear & we are ready to
      receive it & we are.
In a small luminous cabin, atop North America's skull, Nose Mountain,
      Alberta, Canada.

2000

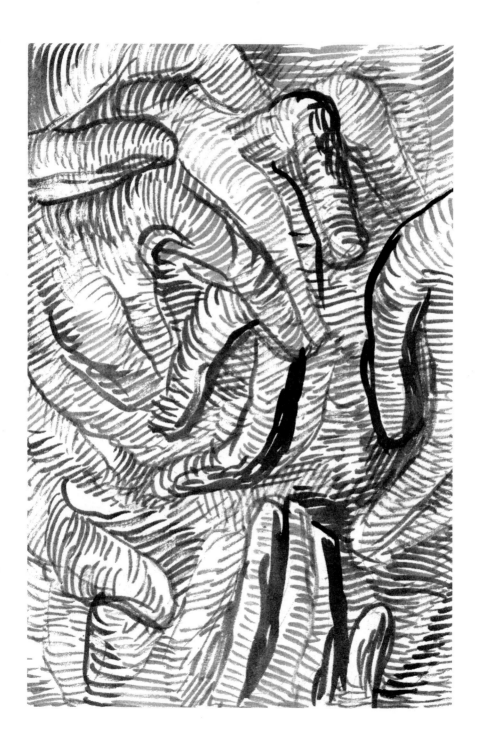

## No ideas but in moving hands

With no ideas for writing, Vivian reminds me at times like this
        to exercise the hand
so move hand—write about how far you are from all the action
        in New York
move hand—write about how nice to get away from Bushisms
        for the week
move hand—like our beautiful fingers moved last night
move hand—faster, so much to be done and such a short
        life to do it
move hand—keep the mama & papa bears guessing
move hand—turn up the Leonard Cohen CD and keep away
        from temptation of those 2 TV stations
move hand—finish yr novel about a homeless outreach center
        director detective
move hand—let the gods know you're not afraid
move hand—swish the air and turn the broom into a stalk of edible corn
move hand—persuade the earth's forests to denounce the Nike swoosh
move hand—age the wine and smile gracefully
move hand—try to imagine a utopia no one has yet written
move hand—even if nobody reads yr poems, the least you can do
        is keep the graveyard at bay

2001

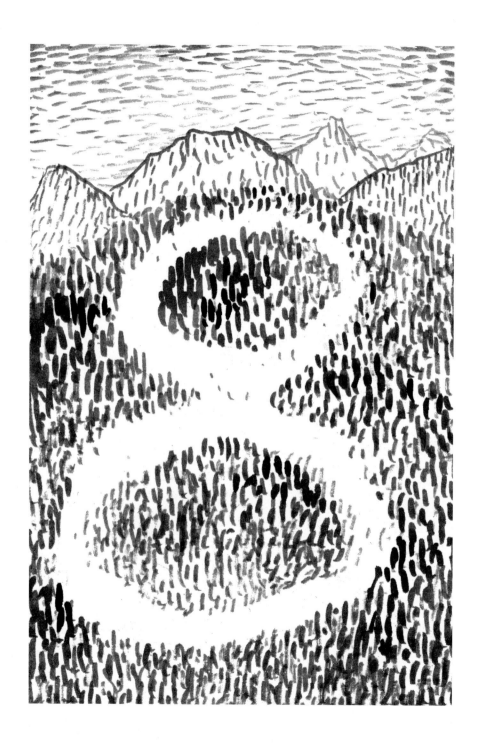

## Walt's Trees

Here in Alberta's forests, the trees honor a long-term peace treaty
In the wind they bow hello to their neighbor trees
They lower branches welcoming new human arrivals to the tower
None defend themselves with guns or night-vision missiles
None have developed high-tech pepper spray for crowd control
None go to Congress every 10 minutes pounding wood tables—
        "give more war money"
In Nose Mountain, no four-star general trees moan over lost suitcases
In distance, I spot clear-cuts, where buzz-saws've carved giant figure 8's
Who would cut down such beautiful herds of leaving breathing organisms?
Walt's trees, will you forgive my daily reading of *The New York Times*?

June 2001

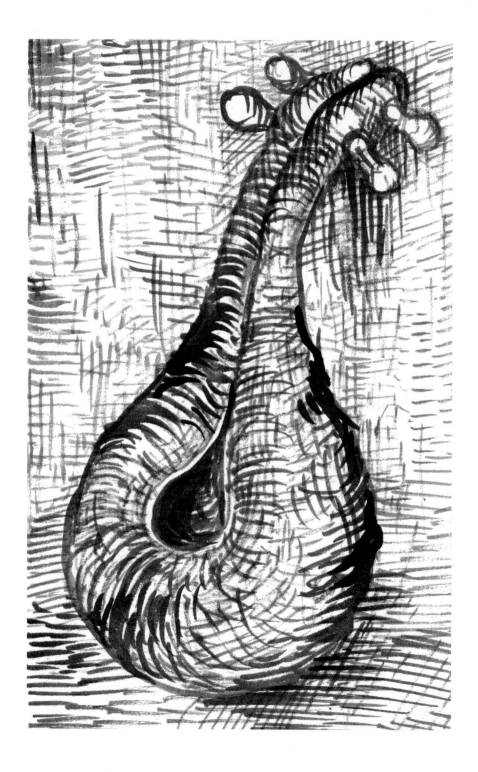

## She Makes My Lute Awake

It's morning in Nose Mountain's pine forest cabin
Outside the elms and evergreens rock, rattle, shake
Last night we read Tom Wyatt by the propane heater
Today the air is pure, & she makes my lute awake

There's a symphony outside made by birds & strings
Forest is grumblin as if ground's about to quake
Baby bears are yawnin & wolves all start to howl
She radios the weather, then makes my lute awake

From bookcase window Sky the Cat studies Sky the Sky
There's a peacefulness up here that string notes amplify
When gods grow sick of heaven they'll retire at Nose gate
Till then, I brew the coffee, she makes my lute awake

She plays some piano, guitar, a swiss trombone
Up here Apollo stood and named the moon
After breakfast in mythic robes we meditate
Then flip back the jazz & make our lutes awake


2001

# Letter to Allen from North America's Skull

Allen, I'm sitting in straight-backed chair
Vivian's Canadian forestry cabin Nose Mountain, Alberta
meditating each morning, sitting up, eyes open, following
        breath thru nostrils
more than I did while you walked this planet,
like you taught me Naropa, Boulder, summer 1980,
though with bad back I need help from this sympathetic chair.

Allen, I think you'd be happy yr younger students & friends
still care to follow yr advice, still write poems imagining your
        editing eyes on their shoulders—
It's beautiful here, with eyes open out cabin window
I can see the tallest evergreen on lawn sway in northern breeze,
can see fog slowly filling horizon,
fog inhaling my exhale, fog carrying my spirit in its hazy pouch
        traversing the continent.

Did you ever think we'd elect a president dumb as GW?
Each evening *The NY Times* has to make key editorial decision
        whether to quote GW's daily linguistic fuckups
or paraphrase instead, perhaps use partial quote ending right
        before tongue slip,
about once a week including on front page a line like:
"Teach a child to read and he or her will pass a literary test."
Did you think thoroughly discredited programs from your lifetime,
        Star Wars and nuclear power,
would spring back to the front burner?—so much of our language
        still taxed by war.

Up here in mountain forests, there are no newspapers,
though we've access to 2 TV channels & a too-slow world wide
        laptop computer web.
I know Milosevic was sent to Hague's war crimes tribunal few
        days ago
but haven't been able to follow his nation's reaction.
I know there were protests in San Diego against genetically
        modified food
but wasn't able to learn details—
I wish you were here to see this new anti-corporate-globalization
        movement grow!

Up here I don't know who's winning at Wimbledon,
don't know whether Barry Bonds continues to hone in on McGwire's
        70 home runs,

don't know who won the Mets game last night or night before.
Allen, I think you would have liked Vivian.
Actually, let me introduce you—
here she is, a meditator, visual arts exhibitor, now writing poems
        & experimental novels publishers promise to read,
long hair, bluegreen eyes, laid back Canadian energy most of the time,
a sharp empathetic mind of a once biologist and still herbalist
        and human rights ecological advocate,
beautiful lover, here taking care of me outside my urban
        living proclivities
during 8-summers stint as Alberta firetower watcher.

So, I'm doing alright—better than most in our nation,
probably 7 million these days without permanent home,
2 million locked away in nation's fastest growing industry—
        prisons,
many for minor pot crimes, or drugs you always viewed
        as spiritual/medical, not criminal, questions,
several hundred thousand families about to be kicked off
        welfare January 2002—
Clinton's promise to end welfare as he knew it—nobody
        on TV talking about this historic safety net rip.

While I'm up here for two weeks breathing clean mountain air
they may be spraying pesticides through NYC streets third
        summer in a row!
Battling flu-like symptoms of West Nile virus, they've created
        a cure worse than the disease!
If you were walking yr Lower East Side haunts after midnight,
you might have to duck quick into alleyways to avoid
        splashed untrained spray trucks!

Allen, we still need you, yr ideas, your imagination, your poetry,
        your presence,
we're trying to honor your memory, trying to keep your compassionate
        activist utopian spirit alive.
When Bush ran for president, he said he was a "compassionate
        conservative,"
misusing one of your favorite Bodhi-politic adjectives—
governing, he's pulled out Kyoto protocols on global warming,
cut taxes on wealthy so no money to fix broken social programs,
reneged on campaign promise to limit CO2 emissions, dropped
        a few obligatory bombs on Saddam,
racing full speed to prove conservative credentials while we wait
        to see what the hell he thinks compassion might mean.
If I figure it out, I'll let you know.

Allen, I miss our once-every-few-months political discussions
        at the all-night Kiev.
Gregory died earlier this year, left another void in New York's
        poetry scene.
If you get a chance, please write, tell me which part of the Multiversal
        Emptiness you're hanging out these days.
Actually, if you can hear me now, you know I don't believe
        in any notion of conscious life after death,
don't buy any of the existing scripts for Heaven, Hell,
        or the Ground Round.
And yet, I write to you, as one writes to the future—
and I remain, your student and friend, E. Katz.


July 2001

# In Defense of Lateness

Sitting at kitchen table, Nose Mtn, ten minutes after breakfast,
        nowhere to go, no work anxiety,
no brochures due Thursday afternoon, no meetings to prepare
        for supervisor at noon—
It occurs to me: where'd concept of deadlines arise?
Isn't a deadline something for the living to avoid at any cost?
As best we know, in our three measly dimensions of space,
        time moves irrevocably forward—
but whoever decided it was thus best to arrive "on time"?
When I enter work late, which is often, why feel so guilty?
Why not put off notions of alarm clocks and tennis shoes?
Why not celebrate the mystery of delay, the not-yet of the not-here?
Why not savor the extra fifteen minutes it takes to depart
        your apartment fifteen minutes late for the train?

Two years ago, a week after injuring my back,
I was 20 minutes late for an informal date at The Knitting Factory
        with a writer whose work I admired.
I looked every left-side profile seated in the bar—none was hers.
When I got home I called to see what happened—
"Now that you've moved from Jersey to New York," she said,
        "you have to learn to show when you say you'll show."
Lucky with sharp jolting lower spine pain to show anywhere at all,
I learned to appreciate the practical beauty of lateness in hastening
        the awareness of incompatible lives.
Perhaps the world is made up of those who slowly observe time
        and those who open their morning eyes on time?
Perhaps there is no real difference at all between on time and late—
        each a temporary malady interchangeable
in temporal dimensions we're simply late in discovering?

Perhaps I was born too late for my own good? I would like to have
        been there for the first jazz poetry reading!
I would like to have driven Mississippi for Freedom Summer!
I would like to have helped levitate the Pentagon!
Would like to have cast 12 million more votes against Hitler
        after the 1920 Kapp Putsch!
Would like to have warned Tyrannosaurus Rex: "Duck!
        Meteor incoming!"
I would like to have procrastinated fifteen minutes before lifting
        that orange juice carton that threw out my back!
I would like to have been healthy enough to march in Seattle!
Perhaps he or she who hesitates wins the day!
Perhaps after quantum physics is perfectly explained the one

who enters last will be seen the first one there!
Perhaps evolution is a big zig-zagging 11-dimensional spiral?
Even if time is progress, lateness may be only an illusory
        superstring membrane wavelength away!

I hereby grant purple stars to all who joined the war too late!
But what if I was nanoseconds late the instant I caught Vivian's eye?
What if I'd been a sideglance late seeing that handgun waving
        out New Brunswick's car window?
What if I'd been so late being born into this world I went directly
        to the next?
What if my alarm clock never rang and there was never another
        wake-up call?
Maybe even age 45 there's still time to learn to be on time
        at least for work and special occasions —
and to remember to be late for the final goodbye?

2001

## What We Don't See

Look at those trees! There are millions of 'em
Where the cat treads lightly
Whatever we don't see is there

A helicopter whirls overhead; we are not alone
Strong winds coerce the leaves into speaking politely
In forests like these, the unseen future flourishes

Millions of species remain undiscovered
Time has its way of dealing with warriors
The trees are doubly upset with the news in the papers

This moment of life is safe from their weapons
Even the radio ends up talking in whispers
Your skin wakes my skin like a million tiny fingers

2002

# To the Northern Winds, July 4th

Sitting in cabin kitchen with Vivian
meditating with eyes open
following breath out nostrils
the day clear and beautiful
but cold, and windy as hell

It's heaven up here in Canada's north country
no inkling of industrial air pollution
not another human being within 50 miles
just Vivian and I reenergizing our love
and daily nightly mercurial wanderings

Forest dust blows from here through the hemisphere
it slips through the eyelid & the screen door
nests between the molars & under the tongue
it can make a nation crazy
or cause a dog to sit up and take notice

It's been a crazy fucking year
full of death and the fear that creates more death
full of heightened alerts & habitual nightmares
full of bedroom intruders dressed in terrorist beards
& talking busted syntax on the Pentagon's porch

O Northern Winds can you blow some uncommon sense
into our nation down below?
Can you wine & dine us this year with a cleansing tempest?
Can you whistle and make our giant egos disappear?
Can you help us elect a new president?

The terrorists have murdered innocent lives
and given America's insane right an unnatural gift
from up here where the winds howl
it's obvious nature abhors a fundamentalist judge
and the whole pyramid scheme of corporate theft

The Northern Winds blow the leaves hard
but take time off so the trunks can rest
We remember the World Wars and the inhuman slaughters
we recall the old famines and the new disease
yet have begun to build another dangerous century

Last night ravens flew figure 8's near the cabin, playing
in yr gusts. O Winds, we have learned to cross large continents

to embrace our love. Can you shake us out of our future-destroying
weaponry for a new start?  Tell the children:
another new century can begin whenever we choose.

2002

## 2001 Skies

July 1st, Canada Day, we sit morning meditation facing out Vivian's
        forest cabin window
today lower back muscles ache, I squirm in chair seeking comfort,
watch a thin trail of smoke rise from sage incense stick on window sill.
Where does that smoke go? Surely to the place where dead souls
        congregate—
Heaven & Hell a myth invented to avoid announcing humanity's
        humble place in the universe.
Follow breath out nostrils, empty thoughts, let spirit enter soul's
        thin smoke stream.
This morning Vivian's & my one-year anniversary,
beautiful dawn of lovemaking before breakfast muffins—
last night white-tailed deer spotted in dirt road by cabin,
easy to see with light lasting till 11pm this far north—
then groups of hares hopping across same road, then marble-sized
        hail thudding cabin roof an hour.
Back to breath, the thin trail of smoke, maybe I should close
        my eyes today?
No, it's our anniversary, all body energies whisper "remain open,"
        how thankful I feel.
Vivian's Siamese cat Sky digs front left claw into my rubber sandal
        near screen door
& starts clopping around the room, 3 tiny paws and one man's
        size 12 sandal—
is laughing aloud considered a meditation faux pas?
Back to breath, back to thin trail of smoke—
a small gray moth clings to window from outside, unable to cross
        transparent threshold & kill itself in the flame.
Inhale, exhale, too many thoughts to empty this morning—
we are not yet anywhere the species we all know we can become.

2001

# The Holy Mountain Texts

In the middle of the Canadian Rocky Mountain forest
We drank woodsy Merlot and prepared to study the holy texts
We read the No Matching Socks Sutra
We danced the Waltz of the Yellow-Rumped Warbler
We recited the Prayer of the No More Royalty Butterfly
We chanted Om My Heart Belongs to You and Yogi Bear
We read the Diamond Sutra of the Torn Moccasins
We prayed to the Humongous Mosquito Gods
We debated the Midrash of Coyotes versus the Pet Cats
We praised the Ghostly Caribou who shed an antler of illusions
We sang the testament of the Back Spasm Healers
We bowed to the white toenails in the Muddy Trail Wolf poop
We meditated on the Front Yard Lawn Mower Sutra
We danced with bees humming in the nectar of bluebells
We marched to the tune of the Double Rainbow Creek
We anointed the nose of the hermetic porcupine
We purified our hairy bodies in the moonlit dew
And yelled "Away ye gods!" as the Holy Grizzly turned.

Eliot Katz and Vivian Demuth
2002

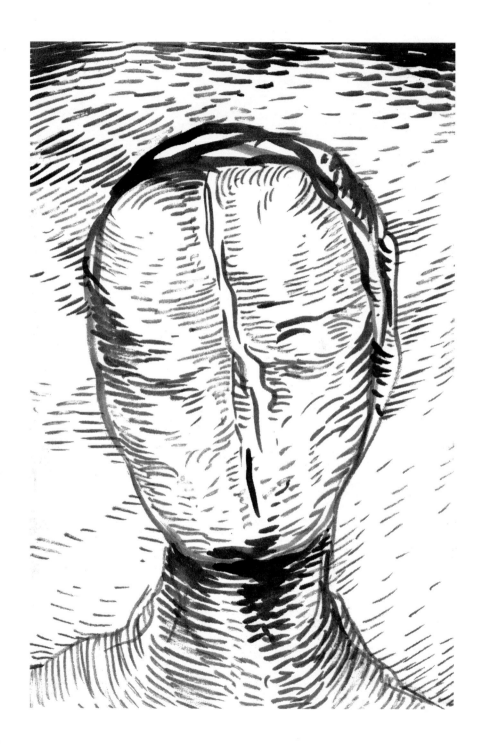

# From Nose Mountain, Love Poem for XMB81

*"Do not allow the kingdom of heaven to wither"*
*— "The Apocryphon of James"*

We light a cedar incense stick & face out
the cabin picture window & glass front door
to meditate. Dharma the cat goes to the
door, stands on her back paws & looks
outside, too. Is it coincidence, or is she trying
to understand the picture we are viewing?
Or perhaps fulfilling her name's sake & joining
us in a reflective journey? Last year Dharma
was a light rambunctious kitten, darting
with sharp paws one end of cabin to other,
running reckless outside after hares twice
her size. This year she is calmer, almost full
grown, and glides slowly. This year, looking
down Nose Mountain's ridge, it's easy
to see the clear-cuts have grown larger
& come closer to the mountain. It is we,
not the gods, responsible to keep this Earth
happily supporting human & other animal life.
The fire weeds & paint brushes are sprouting
flowers purple, blue, yellow, orange, while
below the border a U.S. president & his hack
Congress are sending our ecological work shoes
through a military-made conveyor belt toward
the board room paper shredder. In preparation
for two political party conventions, the dogs
of Iowa have been put on a daily prescription
of amphetamine pills; a pimple unique as a
snowflake or fingerprint has been made to grow
on the nose of anyone living left-of-center Boston
or New York; the unfinished, unworkable
Star Wars laser system has been turned inward
where it can read anti-Bush bumper stickers
traveling at speeds up to 212 political miles
per hour. My love, even though I might complain
a bit about the bites, I would walk thru miles
of West Nile-infected mosquitoes to reach you,
would outrun the mountain lions, beat the bears
in an arm wrestle contest, make the oil rigs stop
their drilling so I can hear your breath at night
& hold you again after too many weeks of sleepless
solitary dawns. XMB81, can you hear me

on heaven's radio? I am calling you from
the innermost part of my being, where the vocal
chords speak in a volume we know but cannot hear,
in a language that has been used since the first
great meteor arrived. There are fundamentalists
born in every nation on this feverish planet,
memorizing false righteousness & uttering fake
compassion. This year the conventions will go
as well as conventions will go. New York City
will see passionate protest and overzealous arrests.
We will work for Kerry in November. As Abbie
Hoffman used to say, sometimes it really is
better to have the lesser of two evils than the evil
of two lessers. It will be another 20 years before
elected officials provide a political solution,
50 before they answer to humane needs. And heaven?
What is heaven? Only those remnants we can
rescue from the extremists' claws.

2004

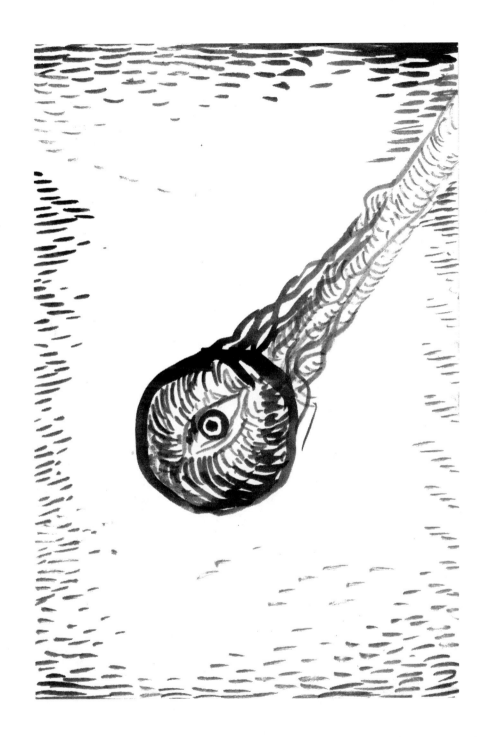

# I Was Tired

I was tired of this war and its bloody gymnastics, tired of seeing denial as the nation's new 24-hour cable occupation. Even the White House door has cracks, I thought, so why not head to the beach for a few days and go surfing, get away for awhile. Only I didn't know how to surf and was never really a good swimmer. What did George W. Bush know and when did he know it? And how long did it take him to forget? So back up to the mountain forests I flew, where it was time for Vivian and I to renew, too long since we last saw each other under New York City sheets, since she left for her annual summer forest fire-watching beat. The war sure drags on, doesn't it, and the images of torture haven't even all been released. One day this war is going to come into our kitchens like Martha Rosler's anti-Vietnam War collages, insurgent Iraqi bullets flying over the morning eggs. Wait, I guess something like that already happened with 9/11, so how did so many Americans get suckered for so long into believing Saddam had something to do with that? I wonder whether Cheney's kids know how to surf? Well, it's good to see Vivian again. My old friends' jazz trio Solar is on the CD player, the Northern Lights are appearing nightly like a Broadway show out the bedroom window, paperback novels and history books are springing out the suitcase & being read, the Buddha dropped by last night for a surprise visit and promised to come back in a couple of days. Even Dharma the Cat can see that more of this wilderness picture ought to be trucked into the city. Last night I dreamt that I was picking stars one at a time off the shelf of the mountain's moonlit sky. Why are they still using those secret prisons & uranium-tipped bullets anyway? Be mindful now, eating those eggs.

2005

# Mixed Nuts With Salt

*"The revolt against redistribution is killing civilization from ghetto to rainforest." —Ronald Wright, from* A Short History of Progress

Here from N. America's skull, it's easy to look down
into the forest & see clear-cuts by day,
up at the sky & see Northern Lights at night.

A deer wanders in bushes 20 feet from the cabin,
coyote calls are heard in the distance unseen—
our species survival may depend this century

on willingness to share rather than ravage.
From up here in the boreal forest, that's obvious,
like wearing boots for the long muddy trail.

In U.S. cities, the world can look more like a ballpark,
in which people simply choose a team
& then cheer, no matter its players' behaviors.

These days, too many Americans are rooting
for the right-wing nuts,
even against the well-being of the planet.

"Go nuts!" urge Limbaugh's & O'Reilly's callers,
"Tear down those trees, let the waters dry,
let Wal-Mart pay its workers in copper coin."

And with home team applause, the nuts are winning.
From up here in the boreal forest, it's difficult
to figure out how to re-write the rules of the sport.

2005

# Who's There?

Here I am, here is a contingent self
a body with eyes and pen
wearing reading glasses this foggy forest morning

Here is what, a contingent what
a being on a mountaintop listening to rains wash in
a disembodied hand to pet the purring cat

Here is death, holding its morning celebration
for it knows another creature will come in just a few minutes
the wind, the fog, wolves howling in the distance

Here is an ecosystem, a contingent planet
Vivian sleeping beautiful under covers in other room
a cat named Dharma that has found a temporary plaything

Here's a kitchen blender waiting for generator switch
a black hole beneath the galaxy savoring its prey
outside window, evergreen outlines becoming visible at dawn

2005

# When the Fire Tower's Jumping

There's a sheet of dark gray smoke
covering the forest's bright orange sunset
and the pre-thunderstorm winds
make the log cabin windows quake

Over in BC they lit a match
to kill a few trees with pine beetles
and the flames took off like Nascar
or like a hard day's night

Ain't had no rain for almost a week now
& the mercury is swelling
scientists say it's global heat stroke
& our elected leaders are so helpless

The fire lookouts are going crazy
Vivian's radio is non-stop gab
The hazard level's extreme & tension mounting
The first lightning bolt's a big drag

Now Vivian's climbing her 60-foot tower
where she's got her scope & forest maps
She's a vision of grace with 20/20 vision
& a sixth sense for tickling sparks

It's been six years, mostly great ones
all the troubles blow away
what's hazard on the mountain
turns to fuel in a city day

When wind dies down & body tires
the U'verse lets out a great big yawn
We're all meat for the planet's harvest
but while we're here we clasp our arms

It's a long hard struggle there is no doubt
I'm glad you're with me for the ride
When wind dies down & planet tires
we'll find a lightning bolt that's ours

2006

# The day of the flies

The whole mountaintop today was abuzz with flies
& I couldn't help thinking of Emily D's poem
about hearing a fly buzz when she died —

Am I dying? Am I like the mouse I saw yesterday
lying in wait for the lawnmower —
me wondering whether it still had breath enough to move.

On CBC radio today they announced Osama bin Laden
had released a second day's worth of internet messages —
why didn't they mention his first day's missive yesterday?

More threats from bin Laden, and I am guessing there
are more boasts in return from Bush, who I'm sure
believes he is winning his ill-defined "war on terror" —

well, we are all going to die anyway — so I suppose
we're all winning — or maybe we're all losing —
or maybe there is a world beyond the contest

where we can watch ourselves watching ourselves,
where the flies buzz & we know we are alive! —
beyond the fear & terror, beyond the businesses

of war. Looking out over the ridge the smoke
from B.C.'s forest fire makes the whole horizon hazy —
I am eating smoke & breathing death, wondering

how much closer are my friends to electing
progressive Democrats or 3rd parties to office, who is
winning Wimbledon, and whether Cervantes was right

in calling poetry an incurable & contagious disease?

2006

47

# Thinking About Emptiness from North America's Skull

*"With no obstruction,*
*How can there be*
*Absence of obstruction?"*
—Nagarjuna, *Verses from the Center,*
tr. Stephen Bachelor

Over the horizon bright
jagged bolts of white lightning
are thrown like javelins
from the top of the continent.

Where are they landing?
Nowhere.
Who is throwing those electrified spears?
No one.

Outside the cabin window after the storm
the tops of some of the mountain's evergreen trees
have become a dirty orange
as if they were everorange trees.

I wonder what natural processes
or acts of industry
have turned the tops of these trees orange?
Is industry a part of nature's course?

From the edge of the mountain
I see dozens of oil rigs dot the landscape
Even three or four years ago
I could only see one or two.

What license from the galaxy
could give oil & gas companies the right
to despoil Canada's boreal forest?
Could a business contract give this right?

Who will stop the logging industry's
ever-widening clear-cuts?
Is it possible that trees exploit us
like this in another universe?

At 11pm, the sun has gone down
and the treetops look green again
What kept me from seeing what was there?
What in this cabin window creates illusion?

With record-breaking heat, the fire lookouts
are on "extreme hazard" all week
They are calling smoke locations into the radio
all day & through the night.

Are there really other humans listening
at another end of the radio?
Who heard Vivian call in that smoky ridge?
If she didn't see it, would someone else?

On the FM radio, I listen to local gossip.
No war talk. The disaster in Iraq must be
over up here! For global warming, the locals
know it's past the tipping point.

At midnight, it finally gets dark
Soon all appearances will vanish
Goodnight Vivian, goodnight Eliot
With luck we'll all meet again in the morning.

2006

## Nose at Night

I'm writing as fast as I can again, one of these prose-poem exercises that often leads to a dead end, but that can sometimes lead to a poem worth typing up back home when I need a reminder to break the mind's exhausted chains. What should I call tonight's meditation on weak-battery'd darkness? Is there going to be any thunder to go along with the flash lightning strikes? Did the full moon bow before tucking itself behind the clouds? The stars have all set themselves into an opaque cup for the night and my mind is racing because I can't think of anything to write about. The moment I close my eyes tonight, I'll surely touch a brain-burning piece of dream heaven. Where did our species go wrong so early in this new century? Why haven't our maps been updated yet? I believe there was a "move forward at reasonable speed" sign somewhere along the road, but our national driver must have missed it. Or maybe one of the Fox News yellers saw it first and turned it backwards? I'm so tired I can't even remember what country I'm in at the moment. Or this moment. Well, the evergreen trees outside the cabin are curling up for a few hours of shut-eye and so should I. Vivian is already under covers and Franklin the Cat is rocking in his chair. Last night, as soon as I closed my eyes, Franklin started jumping all over me & digging in his claws. For now, I'll try to keep my eyes open as long as I can. As long as there are crooks running the country through scare-mongering, a few of us insomniacs might as well keep watch through the night.

2007

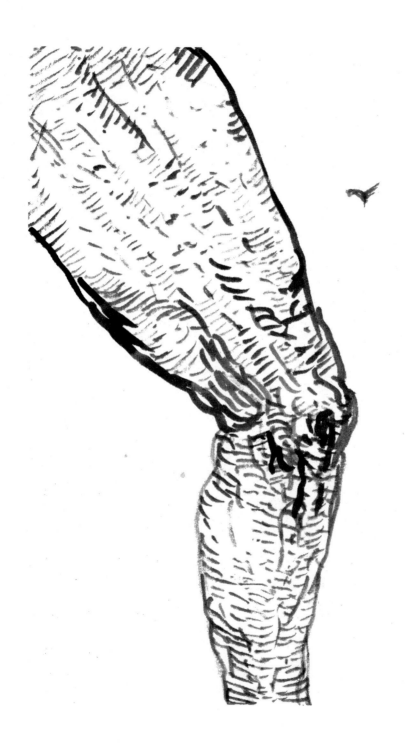

# With Body Another Year Older

Back on Nose Mountain with body another year older
& falling apart. Post-surgery knee is swollen & painful,
making it nearly impossible to walk. Left leg unable
to hold weight of the rest of me, back achy as usual,
but Vivian & the mountaintop beautiful as ever.

This year, a raven has been hobbling along the cabin road
ever since I arrived. Is it a symbol of Poe telling me
death is near? Or perhaps a career as a mystery writer
is near? Or maybe the raven carrying a miniature
recording device & unable to fly away so Cheney
can keep me bugged while I'm out of the country?

Luckily, doctors tell me the knee will heal, and sky
tells me the raven will soon find its circling flock. In long
term, I'm not sure how well this boreal forest will survive
climate heat stroke or pine beetle breakfasts, but hopefully
some of these elder trees will fare better after surgery than
I have. I'll type up more wish lists if I don't die first.

2007

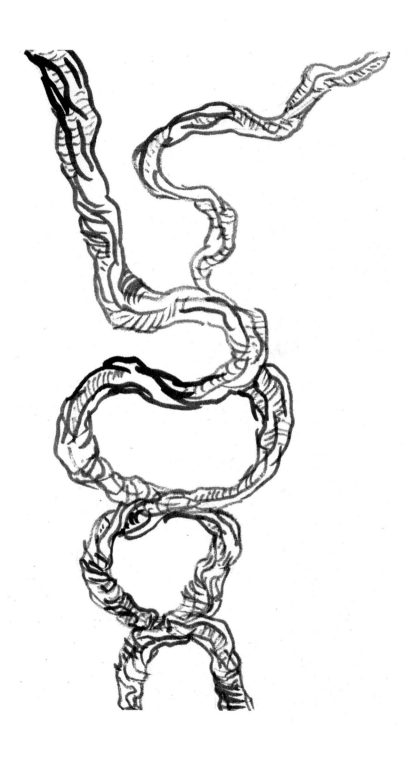

# Breath Is Like the End of Breath

Breath is like incense-stick smoke—
        both trails eventually die off.
The forest trees are like a giant refrigerator
        cooling off the universe.
Bears are like invisible space aliens
        who sneak up when least expected.
Food is like a thermometer—
        best in moderation.
The president is like a pile of wood chips
        burning in anger with a single spark.
Civilization is like a slab of concrete
        wired for unpredictable electricity.
The internet, like a new motorcycle,
        is best driven with helmet & high alert.
Cell phones are like microwave ovens cooking the ear—
        like microwave ovens cooking the ear.
Love is like fleeting love—
        lucky if followed by more fleeting love.
Death is like a down-filled sleeping bag—
        the end of shivering.
All in all, it's a beautiful world
        like the mountain lynx one never quite sees.

2007

# Nose Mountain Rain

The universe is tap dancing on the cabin roof
The evergreen trees are shaking like Fred Astaire's hoof
We're alone up here
on top of the world

It's a chilly summer storm & I'm shivering a bit
Franklin the cat is circling the cabin in fits
I'm reporting from the kitchen table
with a blue-inked pen in my hand

From here on Nose Mountain it's a different kind of news to report
Don't know if the press is hiding from me, or me from it
But I can still feel the war going on
and it's not going well

In 15 minutes Vivian will wake & check her weather
She's got a dozen instruments outside that'll basically say "rain"
The sky's all cloudy
and my post-surgery knee's still in pain

Now Franklin's coming over to say a morning hello
Hey buddy, in the midst of storm, it's good to see you, too
By tomorrow the sun will be out
and my codeine will be through

The beetles in the forest applaud the rain's snare drum
They're deadening the pine trees & the forest's on the run
In the valley, thousands of trees are turning red
It's easy to see the global temperature's on fire

In two days, I'll be flying home to Queens
I hope my knee holds up & customs doesn't give me any jive
There's two weeks' worth of news to catch up on
here's hoping most of the planet has survived

2007

# First Anniversary of the Helicopter Crash

July 3rd, 2007, back hobbling on Nose Mountain
with cane & post-surgery knee on the one-year
anniversary of the helicopter crash that killed
Darcy Moses, 20-year-old Cree firefighter
and father. After 5 years of beautiful nature-loving
& Vivian-loving vacations, last year's trip
was dry lightning, intense heat, endless fires,
& death. Four firefighters were on board
the chopper that mishapped on take-off.
From cabin window, I saw the copter spin
horizontally then fly out of my sights
over the ridge. From her firetower perch,
Vivian saw chopper go down & yelled for help
into forestry radios, whereupon she & I ran
down mountain side to rescue as fast & best
we could. Vivian was stronger & more  knowledgeable
but I did my unhesitant best, running
with creaky back & aging knees & first-aid kit
& fire extinguisher that may have helped
save three lives by preventing downed
helicopter from exploding in flames.

Vivian bravely administered first aid & CPR
on Darcy, but couldn't manage to perform
the impossible human act of bringing back life.
With Vivian and I flown back to town that evening
in different helicopters, today is my first day back
since the crash, and Darcy's family is here
for a one-year ceremony of remembrance,
& a look at beautiful petrified-rock monument
Alberta Forestry has built on this mountaintop
that will now always be Darcy Moses's as much
as anyone's. With a dozen family members of all ages,
including Darcy's mother & three-year-old son,
four young Alberta firefighters in their twenties,
forestry director Don who was first to arrive
by helicopter at crash scene to assist, we are all
standing on edge of Nose Mountain looking down
into a valley of death—with human death mirrored
by a sweeping pine beetle infestation that is killing
large swaths of this ancient boreal forest.

Death—it is your turn to say a prayer and ask
for forgiveness. Leave this grieving family

and this local forestry network alone for awhile.
Even you have to admire the way these folks
fight back, the way they persevere knowing
your jaws are always hanging open just over
the rocky cliff. Let the flowers grow beautiful
over Darcy's monument for ten seasons
before sending your vultures back this way.

2007

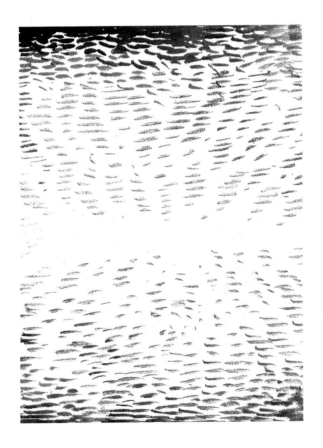

# The View from the Big Woods

About a week before leaving for a 12-day summer vacation, I sent *The New York Times* a Letter to the Editor, which they published on June 20, 2006. In my letter, I addressed an op-ed column by David Brooks in which he wrote that he has a "personal War Council" that believes "success is still plausible" in the Iraq war. I wrote that such a belief simply shows "how callous some of our mainstream policy analysts have become toward the value of individual human lives," since the war had already caused the deaths of up to 100,000 Iraqi civilians and over 2,500 American troops. Little did I know that my partner and I would soon find ourselves in an unexpected position to try to help save actual human lives.

In his book, *The Future of Life*, biologist Edward O. Wilson writes: "It has always been clear that the struggle to save biological diversity will be won or lost in the forests." In terms of slowing down global warming before it becomes global heat stroke, one of the planet's most important forests in need of preservation is Canada's expansive boreal forest, which the Natural Resources Defense Council website notes is "among the largest intact forest ecosystems left on earth." According to the NRDC: "Like the Amazon, the boreal forest is of critical importance to all living things. Its trees and peat lands comprise one of the world's largest 'carbon reservoirs'; carbon stored in this way is carbon not released into the atmosphere, where it would trap heat and accelerate global warming."

For the past 14 years, my partner, Vivian Demuth, has been working summers for the Canadian forestry department as a fire lookout in the middle of the boreal forest in the province of Alberta. For the past 12 of those years, she's been working from mid-May to mid-September on Nose Mountain, a beautifully scenic 5,000-foot peak in the Canadian Rockies, where she lives alone—or sometimes with a cat—in a simple, but solidly built cedar cabin. She has a generator that she can run for electricity a few hours each day, a satellite phone, a propane-powered stove and refrigerator, a radio tuned permanently to CBC, and a TV that picks up rough images of two local stations. There is no fresh water source for many miles. Big barrels below the corners of the cabin roof catch rain water for taking solar-bag showers and washing dishes, and the forestry department drives or helicopters in big bottles of drinking water, along with her food supply, every four weeks. The nearest town, Grande Prairie, is about a 2-1/2 hour ride down a dirt road, so quick trips to the nearest convenience store are totally inconvenient, and Vivian doesn't have wheels up there anyway.

Vivian spends most of her days looking for smokes from inside a 60-foot tower adjacent to her cabin. It is a mystery to me how they either build or truck these towers up to these mountaintops and plant them deep enough into the ground to withstand the wild mountain winds. The network in Vivian's part of Alberta has about a dozen of these tower lookout stations. When a tower person notices a "smoke" (the initial flames of what could potentially become a raging forest fire), she or he uses an Osborne firefinder spotting-scope to try to pinpoint its location. When a second lookout is able to see the same smoke, it becomes possible to identify the exact location by noting the intersecting measured points from the two different scopes. Once the location is pinpointed, a firefighting helicopter or small plane can be dispatched to the smoke to put it out before it turns into a fiery monster that would eat up acres of leaving, breathing organisms in its path.

*Thinking about Emptiness from North America's Skull*

> Over the horizon bright
> jagged bolts of white lightning
> are thrown like javelins
> from the top of the continent.
>
> Where are they landing?
> Nowhere.
> Who is throwing those electrified spears?
> No one.

I'd never spent time in a forest until I started going out with Vivian, a Canadian poet and fiction writer, six years ago. She spends her winters with me in New York City, and once each summer I head up to visit her on Nose Mountain for a week or two. Although the mosquitoes occasionally get under my skin (in both senses of that phrase, especially now that the West Nile virus has reached this part of the continent), and although I sometimes worry about potentially dangerous grizzly bears when I'm walking down the dirt road to throw vegetable scraps far away from the cabin, my previous trips had all been beautiful, relaxing getaways with lots of time for reading, writing, and enjoying the wilderness.

While we met briefly in New York City after a poetry reading, it was Nose Mountain where I traveled in the summer of 2000 to see if it would be possible to start a relationship. In bed on some nights during that first summer, we would sometimes joke that we were looking for smokes. I've written many poems up there, and in those poems I've taken to calling Nose Mountain "North America's Skull." The mountain actually looks like a nose when one is helicoptering in from just the right angle. The view from Vivian's Nose Mountain backyard is stunning, with millions of forest acres visible, although each summer one sees more oil drilling sites in the distance and more figure-8-shaped clear-cut areas engineered by an ever-expanding logging industry. As a progressive poet and news junkie, I do miss my daily fix of Democracy Now with Amy Goodman, commondreams, mediachannel, alternet, counterpunch, a cable talk show or two, and *The New York Times*—I admit to feeling guilty about my daily newspaper habit when I'm in the middle of the forest—but it's amazing how much poetic inspiration one can draw from drastically changing scenery, not to mention taking a few weeks off from a day job.

When I arrived at Nose Mountain this summer, Vivian was in the middle of her busiest fire season ever. Almost every day, the fire hazard seemed to be at "extreme"—the result of too little snow in late winter and extraordinarily hot and dry weather in the spring and early summer. Recent studies show that the increased danger of forest fires is likely the result of global warming, and my sense is that global warming is taking on a mind of its own, attacking those very resources that we humans need to defend ourselves against it. I guess this is the feeling of a tipping point approaching. (Has anyone else noticed that global warming shares the same two initials as our president?) After about a week of consecutive days of precipitation-less heat, July 3rd arrived as a day of lightning strikes and thunderstorms. When lightning strikes in the forest, the forestry radio system turns into a manic talkathon. Lookouts report the instant they see the first strike hit, and helicopters—staffed by a mix of firefighters and forestry department supervisors—patrol the area all day, reporting their take-offs and landings, and letting all those on the area's radio network know what is found at locations where smokes have been reported.

> Outside the cabin window after the storm
> the tops of some of the mountain's evergreen trees
> have become a dirty orange
> as if they were everorange trees.
>
> I wonder what natural processes
> or acts of industry
> have turned the tops of these trees orange?
> Is industry a part of nature's course?

Each fire lookout station has a helipad and a fuel tank. When the helicopters on smoke patrol are running out of fuel, they land at an accessible tower to re-fuel. On July 3rd, soon after a brief thunderstorm had passed, a helicopter came down to refuel at the helipad on Nose Mountain. Vivian was in the tower, and I was sitting at the cabin window watching through some trees. The helicopter seemed to stay on the ground longer than I'd expected, and I figured these guys had been out all day and could probably use a little down time. When it started to take off,

I saw it spin around one time, and I thought that seemed pretty odd, but what did a city guy know? I figured helicopters probably spun around sometimes when they were taking off. A little ballet move, either for practical reasons or just for show. It was about 10 or 20 seconds later that Vivian screamed, and then yelled over the forestry radio: "The helicopter crashed! Emergency! I'm going down! Send help fast!" Or something like that.

I pictured a helicopter crashing with an explosion or fire, so my first instinct was to grab Vivian's fire extinguisher in the cabin and run down to help as fast as I could. With my chronic bad back, I don't think I'd even tried to run at full speed for about seven years until that moment, but I knew that adrenaline would overcome any physical pain for at least a short while. When I got to the edge of the mountain, Vivian was already close to the crash, which was only about 30 yards down the side of the mountain, but it was a pretty steep drop with lots of brush and some poplar trees to walk through or around to get there. I tossed Vivian the fire extinguisher and she yelled to get the first-aid kit and a sheet. I ran back to the cabin, and luckily I'd remembered where Vivian had shown me she kept the first-aid kit. I couldn't find a sheet quickly, so grabbed a thin blanket instead. On that trip or a subsequent one—I can't remember which—I also grabbed a portable forestry radio so Vivian could continue calling her coworkers for help.

At the crash site, Vivian had sprayed the helicopter with the fire extinguisher. Looking back, I'm not sure, but it's possible that this act alone may have helped save some lives. The helicopter was flipped on its side and still smoking, but Vivian was getting into it to help a guy who was seriously hurt in the back seat, and who I couldn't see. Two other guys, the pilot and another passenger, were thankfully walking outside the helicopter; they seemed to be in shock, but didn't seem that badly hurt physically. I opened the first-aid kit, gave Vivian a pair of latex gloves and put a pair on myself. That was about the only thing I remembered from a short first-aid class I'd taken a few years ago. Vivian started calling out for things, mostly bandages, and I did the best I could to find those things in the kit & toss them to her in the helicopter.

I knew Vivian had EMT experience before she was a fire lookout, but I was still deeply impressed by her courage and physical strength, by her knowledge of first-aid, and by her ability to act quickly and decisively in a mountain-environment crisis. And I was doing the best I could for a 49-year-old city guy with a bad back and no experience with this sort of thing. It was probably about 15 or 20 minutes later when a second helicopter landed to provide additional help. I can't really be sure about the time that elapsed—things seemed to be moving simultaneously in slow motion and faster than sound. Soon, there would be a third helicopter coming to help and, I think, a fourth. When the first new helper came down the side of the mountain, he and Vivian somehow pulled the seriously wounded guy straight up and out of the downed helicopter, put him on the ground, and started trying CPR. The pilot had told us the injured guy's name was Darcy, and Vivian was calling Darcy to hear her and stay with us. At Vivian's suggestion, I took a piece of gauze and pressed it against a big gash on Darcy's forehead. I had a strong feeling that I was looking closely into the eyes of the dead or the dying. It's possible that Darcy had passed away on impact, but we weren't sure, and Vivian was doing her heroic best to save his life.

I ran a few steps up the mountain and, again at Vivian's appeal, yelled to the guys still arriving to bring down a stretcher board and make sure a medevac helicopter was on its way. I'll never forget one image I had when looking up at the mountain. One of Vivian's favorite supervisors, Don Cousins, was standing up on the mountain without a shirt, running to help. Don is about 55 or 60 years old, and in winters he races a dog sled up north. So he is probably in pretty good shape. He'd recently told Vivian that he named one of his newer dogs Eliot. It was a comfort to me to know that someone with Don's decades of experience was on the scene, although with the mosquitoes out in full force I wondered why he had taken off his shirt.

Soon, six guys came down the mountainside with a spine board, and they put Darcy on it. I helped put Darcy's arms on the board and helped clamp the straps around him. The six guys carried him up the mountain. Then they came down a second time and went to the other side of the helicopter. Vivian and I looked at each other with surprise. The pilot and the other passenger walking around somewhat in shock had answered yes when we asked them if there were just the three of them on board. Perhaps they had misunderstood us. But now we realized there was a fourth guy whom we hadn't seen, lying beyond our sight on the other side of the copter. When they were putting him on the spine board, he was conscious and even joking, though he said he was fading out a bit. His name was Rob and he knew that something serious had happened to his leg. It turned out that a part of Rob's leg and a part of his arm had somehow been cut off in the accident. I later realized that Vivian's supervisor Don may already have been down the mountainside and taken off his shirt to use as a tourniquet for Rob. I'm also pretty sure that the pilot, who I originally assumed had been walking around in shock, had also been putting bandages on Rob.

When they'd gotten the two guys up the mountain, Don said that a medevac helicopter was at least an hour away, so they were going to take the two seriously wounded guys by helicopter to the Grande Prairie hospital, which was about a 40-minute flight from Nose Tower. The first helicopter off the mountain took Darcy, Rob, Don, Vivian, and the pilot of the crashed copter who seemed in decent physical shape except for a hurt shoulder.

When they left, I was up at the cabin with about a dozen other firefighters, mostly Native Canadians, who'd been flown in at some point to help. All the humans were walking around in a daze and the mosquitoes were going crazy. I figured Vivian would be flown back soon, but instead the forestry department thankfully decided to fly me to Grande Prairie so that Vivian and I could spend the night in a hotel instead of back on the mountain. They gave me about three minutes to gather up a change of clothes for both of us, and sent me right out to the helipad for the flight. I'd been brought in to the mountain by helicopter a week earlier, but I have to admit I was pretty nervous going out so soon after the crash. I remember asking the pilot a silly question—if he could please take his time taking off.

> At 11pm, the sun has gone down
> and the treetops look green again
> What kept me from seeing what was there?
> What in this cabin window creates illusion?
>
> With record-breaking heat, the fire lookouts
> are on "extreme hazard" all week
> They are calling smoke locations into the radio
> all day & through the night.
>
> Are there really other humans listening
> at another end of the radio?
> Who heard Vivian call in that smoky ridge?
> If she didn't see it, would someone else?

The helicopter that flew me off the mountain also carried the fourth passenger, Earl, from the original craft. He still seemed pretty much in shock and there was an ambulance waiting at the airport to take him to the hospital for a check-up. There was also a windowless van. Gwen, Vivian's forestry coworker who was coordinating things at the airport, told me that the van had Darcy's body in it. Darcy hadn't made it. As Vivian and another forestry worker had been trying CPR before the guys had carried Darcy up the mountain, Darcy did not have a pulse. I knew it would have been a miracle to find out that he'd been revived after the 40-minute helicopter flight to the hospital. But it was still a psychic jolt to have his death confirmed.

A guy named Jason drove me by car to the forestry office, where Vivian was waiting for me, and we took a cab to the hotel. I was worried about how Vivian was doing. I knew I felt pretty shaken up, and Vivian had tried so hard to keep Darcy alive. Plus, the tragedy had taken place among her forest worker colleagues and on a mountain that had served as her close friend for 12 years. We held each other a long time that night.

A few days later, on my way back to New York, I saw an article about the crash in the *Edmonton Sun*. It had a photo of Darcy Moses. The pilot, Jack, and Earl had been released from the hospital. Rob, who'd lost part of his arm and leg, had survived and was in intensive care. Darcy was a 20-year-old Native Canadian with a 15-month old son. His mother said he was on only his second helicopter trip, and that he'd told her how much he loved his new job. He said he could see their home in miniature from the air, and he'd assured her just a few days earlier that it was safer in the air than on the ground.

When I got back to New York City, I checked the internet to see if there was any more news about the Nose Mountain crash. There was indeed a new article: the day after the accident on North America's Skull, another Bell 206 helicopter had crashed in a different part of Alberta, killing the pilot, who was bucketing water on a fire and who was the sole passenger on board. As Kurt Vonnegut wrote in *Slaughterhouse-Five*, "and so it goes."

> On the FM radio, I listen to local gossip.
> No war talk. The disaster in Iraq must be
> over up here! For global warming, the locals
> know it's past the tipping point.
>
> At midnight, it finally gets dark
> Soon all appearances will vanish
> Goodnight Vivian, goodnight Eliot
> With luck we'll all meet again in the morning.

I called Vivian every day from New York for the first week after I returned. She seemed to be doing okay. She'd visited Rob in the hospital and said he was in pretty good spirits. And Darcy's family had visited Nose Mountain to do a ritual at the crash site, which seemed to help both Vivian and the family. Vivian had recently finished a manuscript for a novel entitled *Eyes of the Forest*, which included a then-purely-fictional helicopter accident—I think that strange, prescient coincidence had somehow helped prepare her a bit for dealing with the real thing. Now she was back in the tower, back on high hazard, looking for smokes.

Before moving to New York City, I spent nine years in Central New Jersey working as an advocate with Middlesex Interfaith Partners with the Homeless, so I've seen up close a good number of folks going through unfair and difficult times. But there was something different about looking into the eyes of the newly dead on the side of a remote mountain. I have a new appreciation for the risks people are taking to protect this boreal forest that is "of critical importance to all living things." I wish the oil and logging industries would sacrifice some additional profits to match the sacrifice these courageous firefighters and forestry workers are making. And I have a new appreciation for one more area in which the vast resources currently being spent on an unwarranted and disastrous war in Iraq could be put to better use.

July 2006

# II. Looking Under the Hood for the Transition

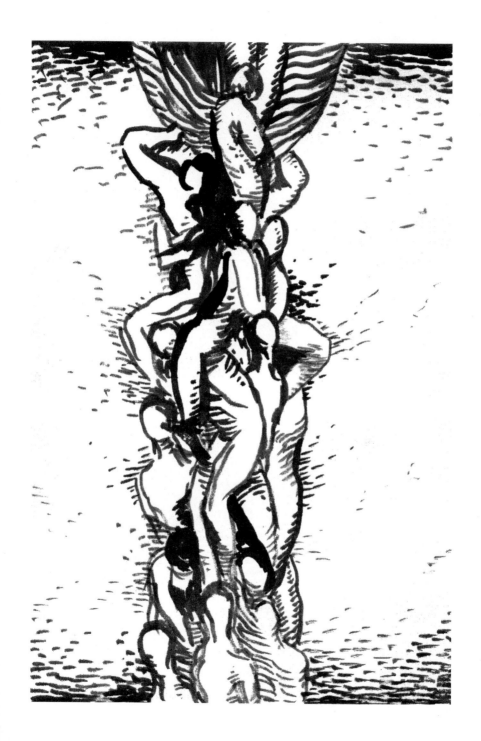

# In Praise of the Seattle Coalition

They came from around the globe to change the shape of the globe
They formed a human chain and sidewalks declared their support
They led labor down unpaved roads and mountain ranges from all sides
        tipped their peaks in salute
They wore turtle caps and the Pacific roared its approval
They chanted "This is what democracy looks like" so that we who could
        not be in Seattle could watch TV & see what democracy looks like
They called for human rights and were gassed with inhuman chemicals
They insisted the food be kept clean of genetic experiment and were shot
        with rubber bullet pellet red meat welts
They demanded an end to worldwide sweatshops and were treated
        to the best nightsticks multinational business could buy
It was a coalition for the ages, of all ages, of all stages, of varying degrees
        of calm and rages
After curfew, the skies lit up & birds flew across continents to celebrate
Ancient redwood trees shook their leaves to prevent WTO delegates
        from being received
The town salmon agreed to wear union windbreakers for the week
When the mayor outlawed public gasmasks, the air sucked up to help out
It was the audible applause of the quantum that drove the police chief
        mad
A dog ran across the road to dispose of pepper spray containers
Stampeding cops were stopped by dolphins swimming in mid-street
        I saw this every hour on the hour behind the CNN lens
In a thousand tongues, even the internet logged on the side of the young
O friends, you have jumpstarted this nation and revealed an America
        with a million human faces
Of course the corporations were defeated, any objective observer
        could see they were outmatched from the opening bell
Now come the subtle somersaults and the internationalist flips
Now the courageous maneuvers that follow a win
Now the flexible glue to keep a coalition together
Now spreading the fun so that more can participate
Now there will be more democracy and then even more democracy
Now you are welcomed heroic at the dawn of a century

1999

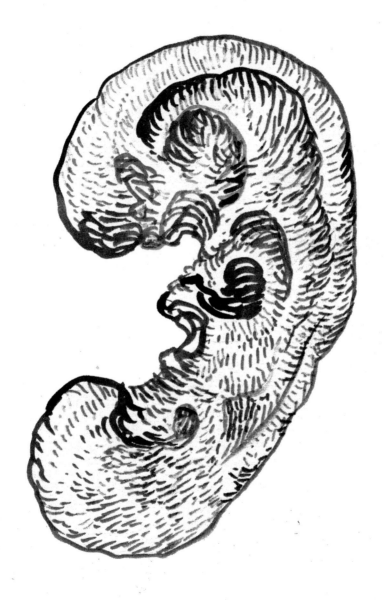

# Cell Phone Special

How would you like your left ear—
well done or medium rare?

2000

# Thor

He was wired, on crack or might as well—
his 3-month welfare motel stay up next week
and he was coming to our office for options.
He settled on one after 10 minutes:
was going to get his gun, blow everyone away
downstairs, at drug rehab center,
then come up to get Lois and me
and finally turn barrel on himself.
No more worries about homelessness, drugs,
no more counselors to answer, cops to fear,
no more god to feel guilty about in morning.
Lois left office suddenly, so this case all mine.
I wasn't sure whether he really had a gun
and if so whether it was on him.
I tried focusing him on healthier
housing alternatives—but there weren't any.
He'd been kicked out shelter for 6 months
and had about used up his 3 months of
welfare emergency shelter motel aid
staying at Route 1's cardboard welfare motel.
More we talked, angrier he got.
I contemplated calling for help,
maybe even the police, but was afraid
if he had gun on him he'd use it right there.
I asked about his family—there was nothing
about family to keep him hooked to this world.
His wife left with son, parents' location unknown.
Just thinking about wife leaving enough
to convince him further murder-suicide
the only honest way out of this fix.
I asked about jobs, what dream job would be.
That angered him cause it required reading
and he'd never learned to read.
"That's easy. I could teach you to read," I said.
"Would you do that?" he asked & started weeping.
"Sure," and we set up a weekly schedule
as he cried all the way out the door.
When he left, I asked his counselor downstairs
to check on him tonight—wasn't sure
that was appropriate social work protocol
but thought it better than calling police.
He never showed up for reading lessons.
When his motel stay ran out the next week,

he threw a brick through window downstairs,
tripping alarm, and sat on sidewalk
waiting for cops to arrive to take him
to only warm bed for which he was still eligible
under Central Jersey's social safety net.

2000

## Rocking the Globe from DC

The cops have boarded up the demonstration's
                central planning space
                    & roped off
      entire downtown Sunday DC
yet, after Seattle, they and we believe
                there is magic enough
    to shut
                    today's IMF meeting
like when three decades ago
              protesters announced
      they would levitate the Pentagon
                    to end America's Vietnamese slaughter
and whether such heavy concrete block lifting
          was possible
                all sides knew odds were high
      it would happen
the U.S. would soon pull out
          & seeds
                  of grassroots democratic experiment
      would implant forever in American soil

I'm standing 7am mid-intersection
                    I Street and 19th
        next to huge pink paper mache World Piggy Bank
            gripping rubber globe in slender jaws
& shitting long silver pipe turds
           staring me between the eyes
              while blocking
      DC's Sunday morning paper route
A dozen video cameras focus on line of young people
              linked arm-in-arm
      some with hi-tech yellow metal sleeves
           their pictures being sent in present time
by independent internet sources
            through as-yet-unbought air waves
      around a pulsing planet
              of overflowing river wires
Tactics built for the forests of the Western Redwood
              are being tested
      in the capital's tarred & feathery streets
           face-to-face afront a line of Helmeted Police
the young are rapping a slow hiphop cadence:
    "No one in

no one out
that's what the line is all about"
200 more milling about, drumming, dancing
chanting Seattle's now infamous
21st century rally mantra
"This is what democracy looks like"
The clouds that earlier looked ready
to keep this event enveloped
are moving to make way for a sun
that's decided to reveal this day to all
The police on other side of ropes & chains
wear million-dollar Star Wars gas masks & knee pads
so are clearly no match for the morning's
idealistic wizardry of youth.


Do these three thousand people working
in small groups
mostly still in their twenties
know what actions this weekend will cost?
How it will endanger/enrich their lives?
tatoo their bodies
electrify their brains
for what part the last century remains?
Do they comprehend this weekend's heavy vows?
Know the DC jails
have a long scratchy memory?
That the World Piggy Bank never forgets?
There is a sense of boldness & empowerment in the air
that tastes as potent
as ginger breakfast tea
inhaled even through hayfevered nostrils
The sidewalk knows it will soon be doused
w/ pepper spray
the store window knows tear gas is on its way
the fire hydrant leaves space
between parked cars
for police nightsticks to crash
upon innocent heads
the prison door hinges are oiled and ready
With no apparent help from pedestrians
the street writes
its own graffiti
to honor the courage on display.

In Saturday's *Washington Post*,
         Police Chief Ramsey remarked:
     "I think we're going to make a lot of arrests
            and ... have a lot of problems"
Last night 670 were surprise-arrested
      marching peacefully
         against the prison-industrial complex
       as if the DC police wanted to do folks the favor
of an up-close-and-personal look
       at the 2-million strong phenomena
    they'd been criticizing
        only abstractly before
Police said those arrested ignored
        an order to disperse
    but the *Post* reported: "even tourists
      who witnessed the event
said not only did police fail
     to order people to disperse
         but they also prevented those
       who wanted to leave from doing so"
A Post photographer & other journalists were arrested
        about which police told press:
      "To the extent we arrested
a person that shouldn't have been, I apologize."

Near George Washington University campus
    21st and H
      a guy in blue suit
        tries to push through the line
The line closes, a mixed group of young people
        long hair, short hair
    shaved heads
      lots of ear, nose, and lip rings
yell "delegate" & create a dense wall
    of arms & torsos
      "No one in, no one out
        that's what the line is all about"
The perhaps-delegate tries pushing with palms
     to no success
     then shoulder first a human battering ram
        at vulnerable knees, yet line holds
He starts yelling phrases I can't quite hear
    & more young people move
      in behind him
       some wearing shark caps or turtle jackets
they start calm-chanting "OM OM OM"

I think Allen would be touched
to know his Grant Park mantra
has filtered thru generational divides
With the help of cops pulling from the other side
this perhaps-delegate finally
smashes his way thru
most perhaps-delegates don't.


The NY Times Monday headline
would read:
"I.M.F. Points to a Big Accomplishment:
It Met on Schedule"
Turns out cops have chauffered
most delegates
through DC's deserted streets
into the meeting at 5am
an hour before activists due on streets
but these young protestors
were blockading
DC intersections by 6am
a sure sign this new movement
can succeed
when new millennium coffee
can brew itself before the sun rises!
A group of cops head-to-toe'd in riot gear
march single-file
up a street center
too goose-steppy for my tastes
About 3 dozen young anarchists
march unblinking
toward the approaching police
they are clad in black pants, shirts, boots
black bandanas covering faces
so cameras won't recognize
they spread across road in few columns
putting bodies in way of police advance
The cops stop & form a single file
crossways
20 feet away from these courageous
crazily provocative kids
The 1/2 hour stand-off is unnerving
violence seems inevitable
yet moving in concert
bandana'd anarchists take 10 steps even closer
a dozen video cameras from news groups large and small
stand between cops and kids

                    awaiting direct footage
                          of bloody confrontation
as another line of riot-geared cops
                    drive up on motorcycles
          to add one more layer
                          of intimidation & rogue support
Young drummers have come around
                          to beat beat beat,
          the big bass drum beat beat beat,
                    the chant: "This is what democracy looks like"
"This is what democracy feels like"
                    then a protection-mantra from the protesters
          to media:
                          "Film them, not us," "Film them, not us"
with whole world watching via World Wide Web
                    the mantra works
                & after 40 or 50 minutes
                          the cops on motorcycles
turn their bikes
                & lead a procession of retreat
                    amid a several column thick
                          communal deep sigh.


A utopian garden party is spreading downtown
                    groups of young women & men
                          block car & foot traffic
          with huge puppets & silver metal sleeves
street theater & dance mocks
          the IMF, WTO, and World Bank
                          there goes a big tooth'd munching
                Structural Adjustment Pulverizer
There a guy in a Clinton costume,
                          there someone walking on stilts
                passing out fake dollar bills
          Signs read "Spank the Bank"
"Get Corporations Off Welfare"
                          "The Debt Kills"
                "Yacyreta Dam Argentina/Paraguay
                75,000 people displaced"
The teach-ins, alternative papers
          new internet sites
                    Noam Chomsky lectures & books
                have taught protesters well enough to know
that IMF & World Bank structural adjustment agreements
          demand poverty-inducing
                          ecologically destructive

capitalist economic policies in exchange
for emergency room million dollar loans
to Developing Countries in need
of both band-aids
and long-term medical plans
The *Washington Post* patronizingly describes protesters
eating from a "chow line
for the revolution"
with trays "piled with cruelty-free rice"
What's wrong with cruelty-free rice?
The IMF ministers are forced
to publicly acknowledge
"a widespread fear"
that benefits of world economy
"are not reaching everyone"
and Monday's *NY Times* front page
sums up our concerns pretty well:
demonstrators accuse "financial institutions
of burdening
poor Third World countries
with crushing debts,
impoverishing peasants, destroying rain forests,
supporting sweatshops & other policies
that, as one sign put it,
'saps the poor to fatten the rich' "
Munch Munch Munch Skin Neck Back
Munch Munch Munch Brain Fingers Genitals
this is what democracy's
devouring ravenous teeth look like.

About noon, a legal rally begins in the Ellipse
buses from around the nation roll in
to a field overseen
by nation's largest phallus
10,000 on lawn hear Roger & Me's Michael Moore,
reps from Students
Against Sweatshops
the Steelworker Union's George Becker—
to demand more humane international economic
& environmental policies,
to shut
the Great Muncher's Bullying Jaw
to march through streets of world's
lone remaining superpower
with signs that read "more world, less bank"
"make global economy work for working families"

By afternoon, a rainy morning has turned 84 sunny degrees
            shut that jaw—
                        through DC side streets
                                    the roving blockades continue
and there are enough www.indymedia.org cameras
                        to record police responding
            with tear gas & pepper spray
                                    arbitrary batons and purposeful bootkicks
Near the end of the legal rally, one end of the Park
                        I saunter to watch 500 protesters
                                    sit peacefully
            while U.S. Park Police sit in steel gear atop scared horses
lined up in a row across one end of the protesters
            A few empty plastic bottles
                                    fly from unseen hands
                        toward the police
until peace-promoting voices from the crowd go up
                        "we're against the World Bank
            not against the cops"
                                    & things calm for 15 minutes
Then police start looking restless
                        & horses begin to shuffle
            the Washington Monument in the background
                                    swallows its Viagra
and SWAT troops begin running thru crowd
            pushing nonviolent protesters aside viciously
                                    one guy swiped by forearm off bicycle
                        face first onto the pavement
a few yards before my eyewitnessing eyes
                        a SWAT cop with name Zarger
                                    on his uniform badge
            smashes a woman's head with nightstick
There is no need for that!
                                    She was trying to move!
            Still cameras start clicking, but there are no news
                        video or film teams around
so young and old alike
            here for the legal rally
                                    are pushed and punched
                        & a single file aisle is cleared
so the park police on horseback
                                    can walk that aisle
            to get to the other side
                        as purposeless as the old chicken joke
only an instinctual urge to smash
                        a few protesters' heads

in one of today's rare in-the-shade moments
away from CNN MSNBC WEB the Sun's gaze
In next day's *NY Times*, a front page photo
will show a similar scene elsewhere:
a young man fallen immobile
under a horse, beaten by a police baton
The caption reads: "Police officers scuffled
with a protester
who fell under horse
on Constitution Avenue yesterday"
Munch Munch Brains Belly this is what the teeth
of corporate-waxed
& glazed
globalization looks like
5:32 pm, Sunday, April 16th, I walk back to metro
as helicopters roar lionlike overhead
while protesters in small park 20th & I
soak tired feet in a small yellow-green fountain.

Monday is the World Bank meeting
Eric, Ben, & I drive to protest late morning
directed by local pirate radio station
amid heavy rains which today don't cease
1,000 people are sitting intersection
while police wearing padded boots
helmets, gas masks, plastic shields
stand semi-circle from one end of block
to other, where snapshot will show
them guarding
a Gap dungaree'd manikin store window display
cops are holding tear gas rifles
& pepper spray containers
while activist drums are banging
the tension is high
there are nonstop negotiations at the line's front
after an hour the cops remove gas masks
& a huge applause leaps out
activists stand up slowly
& begin to cross police lines
in an arranged arrest, about 10 at a time
looks like about 600 placed
into waiting blue vans
the deal enabling civil disobedience
move forward without smashed heads
or bashed elbows & knees
the rain is crashing in dense sheets

84

                              protesters are chanting
"We're here! We're wet!
                              Cancel the debt"
          They are steadfast & brave
                    while the Gap manikins tremble.


In Wednesday's *NY Times*, John Kifner would write:
                    "In the end, Washington was not Seattle"
                              David Frum op-eds:
                    "So Round Two of the great mobilization
against globalization ended in a squelch
                              rather than the photogenic violence
                                        of Seattle"
          The Paper of Record tries so hard to be negative
that any reader
                    with between-the-lines reading glasses
          knows something historic
                    has taken place
that although the World Bank met
          the lobbyist corridor was closed
                    banks shut
          world attention focused on issues
of international trade and finance previously hidden
                    behind back stage corporate curtains
                    just one week earlier—
          even the *Times* front page April 18th admits
"The world's top financial officials
          trying to show sensitivity to poverty
                    as protesters braved a chilling rain ...
                    pledged to pay more attention
to globalization's victims and to commit 'unlimited money'
                    to fight AIDS in poor countries"
          In an unusual moment
                    The *Times* put our general analysis
succinctly on its front page:
          "The protesters accuse the World Bank and the I.M.F.
                    of spreading the gospel
                    of free-market capitalism
to benefit corporations
          while ignoring the environmental impact
                    of their policies
                    and worsening poverty in many countries"
This was not Seattle, but the continuation
                    of Seattle's legacy fulfilled
          successful, theatrical
                    inventive, fun

empowering for a new generation of activists
                    growing smarter
          all the while with video cameras
                              & poetic notebooks rolling
out on the streets no longer letting
                    the mainstream media
          monopolize the whole story
                    the historic lessons are being learned —
one sidewalk curb at a time —
                    a new magic spell has been cast —
          A person walks down 21st Street wearing
                    a red box over her or his head —
in magic marker is writ
                    "Light of Possibilities"
          a yellow bumper sticker across the box says
                    "accountable governance"
a nearby sign reads: "We're not going away"
                    another: "Dissent cannot be shot down or arrested"
                    I was there to witness
          the ground beneath the bank begin to shiver.

                              2000

# The Coliseum's Judges

The Coliseum's judges have been disrobed
of their nonpartisan remnants.
They no longer need reasons,
just the will to reason.
Watch your neck, five wild swords
are unsheathed
        & swinging wildly.

2000

## Alchemy

They've done it—invented some old machines
able to turn a Gore vote into a Bush win
with only a few hanging chads left to show the children.
It's tough to make love while Republicans
prognosticate an obnoxious assembly line—
      but we manage.
They haven't learned yet how to take away
this full body vibration of exquisite moan.
Meanwhile, the hacks are in the back room
      with the Unpresident
devising all night new ways to Undo the Done.

2000

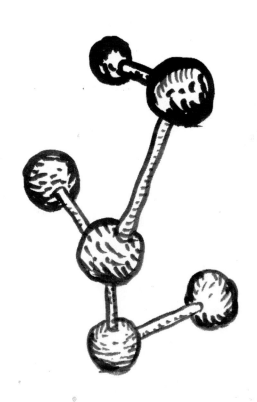

## When a Double Negative Isn't a Positive

Overheard on West Broadway,
a young woman to a male friend:
"I'm the same way,
but this time I gotta tell yuh—
you ain't gettin none tonight."

2001

# Gregory's Last Lines

He was a poet of silk and the shredding of silk.
No earthling nor deity remained immune from his probing questions.
When the academy turned its head for a pulitzer second
he slipped an enlightened humor worm into the gut of poetry
        that hasn't yet wriggled its way out.
With fountain pen tears he mourned the nationalism of the nation
        even as he hosanna'd the home run.
He fooled death, coaxing it into the soup of life
        every time but for one.

Writing in "Many Have Fallen" about American soldiers
        marched by Army into radioactive bomb blasts
Gregory wrote: "All survived / ...until two decades later
when the dead finally died" —
a last line of stunning poetry enough to make the top
        of Emily D's head pop off.

In 1983, Andy Clausen brought him to carouse
        our New Brunswick bars.
We stopped at my kitchen table electric typewriter,
        where Gregory pulled his pocket notebook
and tapped out a piece for *Long Shot* magazine.
The poem was called "Delacroix Mural at St. Suplice."
Deep into typing, Gregory stopped & asked
        what thought I of his last three pencil'd lines.
I eyed his notebook, said I liked 'em but not as much
        as the rest of the poem.
I thought he might write three new lines on the spot—
but instead he stood up, waved his left hand suavely
& declared the poem done at what'd been
        the fourth-to-last line:
"I know the ways of god / by god!"
He knew how to end / at the ending.

I had the chance to read him "Ode to the West Wind"
        on his cancer bed:
"If Winter comes, can Spring be far behind?"
After approaching mortality's last breath in summer,
        he arose to see another new year.
Now, I hear his ashes will be buried in Rome's cemetery,
a neighbor of Shelley & the one whose name is writ in water.
In "Getting to the Poem," Gregory ended:
"I will live / and never know my death."

Who can say whether he was aware of that golden moment
        when the breath says "no"? —
but he damn sure got to the poems.

Death, Gregory knew your secret name,
he knew your habits, your weapons, your games—
now give his verse the life it deserves
        & do what you will with his gilgamesh hair

2001

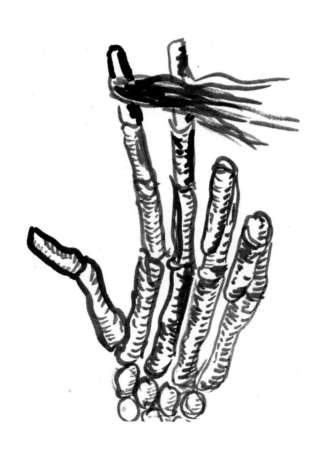

# Recalling Allen

The world could sure use Allen Ginsberg's sane voice and political vision today. Lucky for the planet, his voice is still with us—in books, recordings, and recollections.

Allen was a generous teacher and friend. I met Allen late one afternoon in the fall of 1976. I was drinking coffee, or maybe it was beer, with my roommate Danny Shot, on our Guilden Street, New Brunswick, NJ front porch. We were taking a Rutgers University class on "The Beat Tradition in American Literature," taught by an inspired grad student, Bob Campbell, and we were anticipating a Ginsberg student center reading later that night. A taxi drove up to the apartment across the street where our friend Kevin Hayes lived, and Allen got out of the back seat and started unloading cardboard boxes from the trunk. Kevin was a local poet and friend who was—previously unbeknownst to us—the organizer of the night's event. Danny and I went to help unload cartons that turned out to be Allen's father's manuscripts stored until that night at the Rutgers library.

After the reading, Kevin asked if I could drive Allen and his boxes back home to Manhattan in my orange Chevy Vega, my car at the time being an unexceptional example of one of the worst American car models ever made. Driving around lower Manhattan with Danny and Kevin, Allen guided us on an informative automobile tour of the historic East Village, pointing out landmark sites where famous writers and agitators like Leon Trotsky, Thomas Paine, Emma Goldman, and Abbie Hoffman had lived, worked, or bought egg creams. Allen told us that night he did his best to answer all of his mail. So weeks later, following Danny's lead, I sent a few samples of my earliest poems. Allen responded kindly, taking about ten lines of my verse and suggesting clarifications, deletions, and condensations that might improve the work. He also suggested reading particular books by Williams, Pound, and Reznikoff. Walt Whitman's "Song of Myself" and Allen Ginsberg's "Howl" had been the two main poems that turned me on to poetry, that made me realize how energizing and relevant poetry could be. I was amazed and grateful that this world-renowned poet would take the time to offer thoughtful advice to a young poet he had barely met.

In the summer of 1980, having written poetry for about four years now, I applied for a one-month apprenticeship with Allen at Naropa Institute in Boulder, which is probably where Allen would have remembered meeting me. There, I typed his difficult-to-read handwritten manuscripts and helped go through some of his correspondence in exchange for valuable suggestions about my verse. Although my poetry at the time wasn't very good, I think Allen appreciated my activist instincts. I think he also liked that I was a Jersey poet who had studied William Blake with Alicia Ostriker at Rutgers, since he himself had been using the version of Blake's *Complete Poems* that Alicia had edited, along with Alicia's endnotes, to study Blake. As Allen's apprentice, I had opportunities to see up close his principled commitment to opposing injustice, and his extraordinary desire to help young people striving to create a more peaceful and democratic future. In my work, I would open letters from activists working on a range of issues that Allen was supporting, from ending homelessness in the U.S. to promoting free expression in Eastern Europe. When a Boulder group asked Allen for permission to use an old poem on a poster for an upcoming rally against the impending reintroduction of military draft registration, Allen instead wrote a new poem especially for them, called "Verses Written for Student Antidraft Registration Rally 1980." With humorous imagination, the poem redefined courage as a pacifist trait: "The warrior never goes to War / ...only helpless Draftees fight afraid... / The warrior knows his own sad & tender heart, which is not the heart of most newspapers / Which is not the heart of most Television—This kind of sadness doesn't sell popcorn." How relevant this poem sounds now, during a disastrous and unwarranted war in Iraq, a war whose path was paved in part by a complacent mainstream news industry relaying with too little skepticism the Bush administration's false claims about weapons of mass destruction in Iraq.

At a young poets' midnight reading during a 1982 Naropa celebration of *On the Road*, Danny Shot and I opened up for one of Allen's favorite younger poets, Andy Clausen. Allen attended the reading and, recognizing that my poetry had improved, grew supportive of my work. Around that time, he donated poems and a portion of a reading fee to help Danny and I start *Long Shot* literary journal, to which he consistently contributed original work up until his death. Over the years, he recommended my poems to journals, nominated me for a PEN younger poet's award, and invited me to open up for him at some nice readings, including one that also featured Gregory Corso at New Brunswick's Kirkpatrick Chapel. He wrote an introduction for my first book, *Space*, and offered to write one for my second, *Unlocking the Exits*, which helped convince Coffee House Press to publish the book. He sent postcards from his travels and answered letters and questions about poetry. Since he was one of the busiest writers on the planet, I was always conscious of how generous it was for him to prioritize spending considerable chunks of time supporting the work of younger poets.

Like all good teachers, Allen was also a perpetual student, always thirsty for more ideas and information, and always curious about what his friends were reading. I remember him asking me once while we were walking around the Lower East Side to tell him about the theoretical debates I'd been reading between Brecht and Lukacs around questions of literary modernism. While he appreciated spontaneous energy in the writing of poetry, Allen also had some great ideas for editing, including picturing respected teachers or friends looking over one's shoulder to give their opinions. Allen said that he would often imagine what Kerouac, Corso, or Burroughs might say about the lines of a new poem, and that would help him see his own lines in a new way. I will always remain thankful for Allen's personal kindness and literary support, and I still keep Allen as one of those pairs of editing eyes hovering over my shoulder looking at a new poem.

In addition to spending time advising on poetry matters, Allen was also giving with his assistance on activist projects. In my own case, I think/hope he appreciated that I tried to keep my requests for favors to a minimum. Here are just a few of the efforts I remember to which Allen lent support: He participated in an antiwar reading that I organized at the Nuyorican Poets Cafe during the 1991 Gulf War. When the NJ Anti-Apartheid Mobilization Coalition, led by a terrific Central Jersey activist Valorie Caffee, organized a campaign to press a national arts group to move its New Brunswick convention out of a hotel owned by Johnson and Johnson, which was then the largest U.S.-based company that refused to divest from apartheid South Africa, Allen endorsed our campaign and opened his rolodex for us to look up other key phone numbers and addresses. Long before the internet, Allen coordinated his own version of a Worldwide Web of Poets, Activists, and Alternative News. In February1988, to help us draw more student activists from across the country, he came down to read with me and another New Brunswick poet, Cheryl Clarke, at a convention at Rutgers, where we were hoping to start a new national student activist group modeled after SDS. At that National Student Convention '88 reading, with our conference's main advisor, the late organizing genius Abbie Hoffman, in the audience, I remember Allen cautioning a new generation of young activists to learn how to separate opposition to government policies from any anger they might feel toward their parents. I took this advice as meant both literally and metaphorically, that activists should deal with their personal emotional issues outside of the movement so that unresolved psychological conflicts wouldn't interfere with attempts to develop sane and effective political strategies. After having watched sectarianism and violent tactics hinder some segments of the 1960s U.S. student left, Allen was eager to help a new generation of activists build on the previous era's strengths and avoid repeating some of its mistakes.

In the mid-1990s, with Bill Clinton moving the Democratic Party away from its liberal traditions and toward the political center, and with Newt Gingrich engineering far-right Republican victories with his "contract with America" that many of us were calling a contract on America, Allen began asking poet friends around the country for poems addressing those deteriorating times. (Little did we know how much worse things could get only five or six years later!) Allen spoke to me and to Andy Clausen quite a bit about that project, and after Allen's death, his longtime assistant Bob Rosenthal invited Andy and me to complete the collection Allen had nearly finished, initially intended for *The Nation* magazine and eventually released in 2000 as a book called *Poems for the Nation*, published by Greg Ruggiero's Open Media Series at Seven Stories Press.

Prevailing cultural mythology says that 1960s radicals became more conservative as they got older. Along with thousands of known and unknown organizers from that era who continued to display long-term progressive commitment, whether by public activism or private lives spent in professions like social work or education, Allen's life and work help put the lie to that myth. Throughout the years that I knew Allen, his social-activist commitment never wavered; he only grew better able to explain his thoughtful, progressive beliefs in clear, lively language that was usually difficult for open-minded people to dismiss. (Take a look at his later interviews in *Spontaneous Mind* to see what I mean.) Along Shelleyan lines, I think it would be fair to say that Allen Ginsberg was an important democratic conscience of Cold War America—often unacknowledged by the mainstream corporate political pundit class, but probably more well known and influential during his lifetime than any other poet who had come before. He set an inspiring example of how to combine a literary life with principled social engagement, spiritual concern, and personal integrity.

Today, we are back in a time that in many ways resembles the era Allen described in "Wichita Vortex Sutra" when "almost all our language has been taxed by war." The George W. Bush presidency—accompanied by a Republican-controlled Congress and a conservative Supreme Court—has been a fiasco both at home and abroad. Since the atrocity of September 11, 2001, the Bush administration has been cynically able to manipulate American fears to promote an unpopular menu of right-wing proposals that were largely on their to-do list from the moment they took office: from tax cuts for the wealthy to the deadly and illegal war in Iraq, from domestic spying and conservative judicial appointments to eco-destructive industrial policies. Also worrisome is the expanding right-wing TV and radio talk-show circuit that has been at least partially successful in marginalizing dissent by accusing those who vocally disagree with Bush administration policies of being "unpatriotic." Thankfully, as I write this piece in March 2006, the American people in growing numbers are finally beginning to see through the Bush adminstration's rhetorical smokescreens, and Bush's approval rating has dropped to the low 30s. Now, if we could only figure out how to effectively translate these growing progressive energies into a new, more humane policy road for America.

In 1965, Allen had suggested that a Berkeley anti-Vietnam War rally be made more theatrical, and offered imaginative ideas to make that happen. (See "How to Make a March/Spectacle" on p. 9 of *Deliberate Prose*.) Those suggestions influenced some key rallies of the 1960s antiwar movement, and one can see their continuing influence in contemporary activism by taking even a cursory look at the theatricality—the huge puppets, the creative signs, the dancing and drumming—of the global justice protests beginning with Seattle 1999 and the recent international protests against the Iraq war.

With an astonishing literary imagination, an original sense of poetic forms and rhythms, a unique mixture of humor and historical insight, and an extraordinary ability to show the interconnectedness of various aspects of our emotional, spiritual, and political lives, Allen energized Poetry to give his work a sense of timelessness that I think really will make it "good to eat a thousand years." Certainly, fifty years after "Howl," Allen's poetic and activist legacies continue to move young people to believe that, as the global justice movement puts it, "another world is possible"—a world with much less poverty and war, with far cleaner air and water, and with a deeper commitment to civil liberties, civic participation, interpersonal cooperation, and democratically accountable social institutions.

2006

# III. When the Skyline Crumbles:
## Poems for the Bush Years

# When the Skyline Crumbles

Was sitting Astoria kitchen chair about to vote mayoral primary,
then would've hopped subway to work Soho's Spring Street —
turned TV on for quick election check when CNN switched
        to picture of World Trade Center #1
with surreal gaping hole blowing dark smoke out a new mouth.
Witnesses still in shock were describing a plane flying
        directly into the building's side
when a second plane suddenly crashed Twin Tower 2
and orange flames & monstrous dust rolls began replacing
        the city's world renowned skyline.
Soon the city's tallest buildings crumbled, one at a time —
with 50,000 individual heartbeats working in Twin Bodies,
        it was clear this horror going to be planetfelt.

I stared stunned at TV another half hour, called Vivian working
        Canadian summer forest job to assure I was physically okay
& mourn together, then wandered my Queens neighborhood —
almost everyone walking mouths open silent, eyes unblinking.
Two women & two men on 31st Street cried into cell phones,
        trying reach loved ones working the WTC,
a mover moaned Age Old Prophecy to his buddy loading the van:
        "The world has changed, bro."

Wednesday I subway'd into Manhattan looking to volunteer
        with bad back,
only found location to leave a donation check, all other slots
        remarkably filled for the moment —
also wanted to sense the air fellow Applers were breathing,
smoke that torched bodies now tangibly coating tongue &
        nostrils, dust burning all 3 eyes —
7th Ave above 14th St almost empty rush hour so our dead
        could be counted, a clear road to the next realm,
perhaps a friend's friend miraculously uncovered alive,
        given space to speed St. Vincent's Emergency Room.

Thursday I sat half-hour Union Square with a Tibetan group
        meditating for peace
as mainstream TV helped lubricate America's war machine
        hosting Flat Earth hawks urging 80% toward retaliation
against bin Laden or any country harboring bin Laden's cells —
even as academic analysts noted moments before those cells
        now spread to 30 countries including U.S.
Fox News had hosted a discussion between the far right

      & further right —
Newt Gingrich: The terrorists should be found & crushed —
Jeanne Kirkpatrick: We already know who they are, why wait —
a procession of military experts advocating carpet bombs & napalm.


On Friday night, 3000 New Yorkers, mostly young,
      candlelit Union Square
to mourn the victims & stand for peace with signs like:
      "War Is Not the Answer" &
"Honor the Dead; Break the Cycle of Violence" —
CBS-TV covered the event as another cute show of
      the city's spirit of togetherness
sandwiched between two dozen stories of a flag-waving public
      meat-hungry to support Bush Jr's rush to war.


After years of U.S. missiles flying into outward shores,
a decade after dozens of thousands of Iraqis cruise missile'd
      to death under Father George
the war has now come home, where it's apparent to all
      what a senseless random murderer
      is the one-eyed giant Terror
how it eats its innocent victims screaming alive, feet flailing
how it breaks the strongest of backs, rips flesh wide open
how it tosses arms East, legs South, skull & genitals
      North & West
how it forces hardened athletes to dive head first 99 floors
      to a concrete death softer than its iron teeth
how it leaves no paperwork behind to comfort the living
how it answers pleading mothers & weeping babes
      with a knife to the belly, glass shards to throat
how it burns a skyline of fresh bones to fragile white ash.


Now, we walk memory's long marathon to honor our dead;
now we watch a million New Yorkers work courageously
      to meet the initial test,
daily tasks small to heroic, delivering socks, pulling two-ton girders
      off fallen firefighters atop creaky broken floors,
ignoring fear everpresent, unknown particles filling the air.
Now we see whether Americans can meet the next human challenge:
Protect the innocent & reject Terror in all its disguises,
      even strutting on TV in our own leaders' garb?
Or merely act a mirror of its latest highrise profile?
The sometimes bitter juices of justice, law, human rights, & peace?
Or shot after shot of eternal bloodthirst?


                mid-Sept. 2001

# The Logic of War

1
A group of Bush Sr's US-armed
fundamentalist freedom fighters
compared to our own founding fathers
have become Bush Jr's evildoers
who need to be smoked from their caves—
and the *National Review* philosophers
say postmodern theory has wrecked
            the planet with relativism?

2
How come if we stop shopping
            the terrorists win?
But if we create a million hungry refugees
            through bombing
                  the terrorists haven't won?

3
Because the World Trade Center was attacked
any Bush-initiated response is considered beyond reproach.
Locked in the Language of War, it's impossible
            to find another way out.

4
We are fighting to preserve freedom
a cause so important almost no dissent
            can be televised

Where's the discussion in mainstream press whether
investigations, intelligence, freezing assets, police action arrests
plus a more democratic egalitarian foreign policy
            would have been more appropriate
                  and effective in the long term
                        than war?

5
Although a person's terrorist links may be as-yet unproven
            he or she may be denied a civilian trial
given a military tribunal exclusively for terrorists
at the sole discretion of one who stole highest office
            with the help of five civilian judges.

6
A 15,000-pound bomb is called a daisy cutter


7
Every day ticker tape moves across bottom
        of CNN's screen
updating the latest estimate of WTC missing
        presumed dead
                now hovering around 3,000.
Each day *NY Times* features an obit page
        with individualized moving stories
                of victims of 9/11's inexcusable horror.
Through tragedy described on personal level
        we are learning the Preciousness
                of Each Human Life.


Bin Laden on videotape gloats heinously
        over high American civilian death counts
                he calls blessed terror.
Every day we are learning which human lives
        are precious to whom.


A New Hampshire professor has completed a study
        estimating over 3,700 Afghan civilian deaths
                from U.S. bombs.
Not a single mainstream NY paper or TV station
        covers this study or derives
                their own tally.
Each week I see one or two articles on the web
        about starving freezing refugees
                forced to flee the bombing—
300,000 shivering in Maslakh, 100 dying each night,
        230 buried in Dehdadi, mostly kids
                judging from small size of burial plots.


The Pentagon says it is pointless to attempt verify
        Afghan civilian deaths.
Every day we are learning that the value
        of human life is relative
                to how many steps removed one feels
                        from the dead one's relatives.

8
On Fox News, Bill O'Reilly says Afghans
        are responsible for crimes
                of their government.

Does anyone remember Vietnam?
        Blessed terror of the Nicaraguan Contras?
                Angola's Unita? Salvadoran death squads?

Thankfully, no other country's military
        blamed me or my friends for those.

Didn't the U.S. cold war government help create
        the cave tunnel training camps
                for which Afghans are being bombed?

One of these centuries leaders on all sides will learn
        to leave the gods and people out of it.

9
Our newest ally Pakistan supports terrorists
that have stormed India's parliamentary gates.
The U.S. sensibly urges India to show restraint.

10
Those who remained in cities, & survived, celebrate.
In a refugee camp, a mob has beaten Robert Fisk,
only major Western journalist in country
        writing against massive bombing
because he looked Western & didn't speak their language
        & his driver looked like George Bush.

I protested the war as a risky gamble with millions
        of innocent Afghan lives
but understood this one had more justification
        than Vietnam or Iraq
and am quite happy to watch the fascist Taliban flee,
        music being played,
& women walking Kabul's streets w/o burkas.

11
What idiot wouldn't realize terror attacks
would be a gift to the American Right
as well as mass murder untold sentient beings?

If the terrorists attacked mainly because
        they don't like our individual freedoms—
then by supporting the president
        in all his foreign & domestic policies
don't we let the terrorists win?

For now, we are teaching the terrorists a clear lesson
that you don't solve your gripes with bombs
unless you're the world's only superpower.

                                        Oct.-Dec. 2001

## The Basic Elements

Turned 45 while low back spasmed first time in few months—
body getting old, but at least concepts of life
        becoming clearer:
everyone on planet has 3 basic needs:
material (food, water, shelter, medical, solid spot of earth);
spiritual (creativity, religion, therapy, meditation, love, purple skies);
empowerment (via elections, movements, razor blades, or bombs).
Sex overlaps the categories & humans rarely choose
        the healthiest alternative in any field.

Deep in their heart everyone knows 2,000-year-old concept
        of a sole omnipotent god
        is a fiction centuries outlived.
What keeps monotheism alive? Some say fear of afterlife—
I think fear of censure by other human beings for revealing
        what lies deep in the heart—
one's honest skeptical thoughts thrown aside
        for sake of church, mosque, temple, TV news picnics—
and thus thousands still die every year for praying
        to a god with different sized shoes.

We've known long before Argentina that IMF austerity
        will not solve globalized poverty
and yet defenders of a free market that isn't free
        still fill all our top op-ed pages.
As for the bombs used when Democracy's Highway blocked,
everyone now understands that's a problem—
        when it's others doing the bombing.
Life on the planet is obvious
        but not in the same way
        to any two folks—
that's the challenge of building love
the dilemma of a world growing colder
        even as global warming infiltrates our core.

                    2002

# The Weather Seems Different

It is snowing in Athens tonight & Apollo with ice in his beard
        is having a difficult time singing
About six twin engine miniplanes have crashed coast to coast
        in empty fields & a Bank of America building
My love, you know that death is both a separation
        and a permanent glue
You know that I am the son of a patient duct tape expert
        and the daughter of a wine never allowed to age
Love, we are all things to each, we are needy in just the ways
        each other needs but doesn't yet comprehend
In the open fields of Somalia there are civilians running circles
        freaked out shivering they might be next
From a satellite 10,000 miles above earth, like an empty chair
        with telescope
a disembodied human eye stares at us & stares at Colombia
        he is looking below the oceans for new caves
He is looking for people who are not yet in favor of empty chairs
        placing nuclear-tipped dynamite in empty caves
The danger is real, one can feel it in the air
        even if unsure from which directions it is borne
We are all getting older, we have realized this year it's time
        to get serious about ducking death's temporary wings
Time to get our 10-dimensional affairs in order; between your
        big toe and its chipped nail
there is a fire-breathing vulture just waiting for the dimensional wall
        to collapse even for a millisecond
History repeats itself but sometimes as a young student pilot
        unsure how to create an effective farce
My dear, the vulture escaped for my birthday last night
        it was in our bedroom pecking below the sheets
It has eaten us alive and regurgitated us back into this world —
        time will tell whether we are healthier than before

2002

# Typing on Terror Alert, Memorial Day

Back in my younger days, I would have nights like this,
sitting down at the typewriter, body energies churning,
but no inspiration, nothing that might even pass for an idea.
So I'd go out, head to the bar, drink a little tonic with my gin,
happy to know that other nights would come
with subject matter presented in outstretched hands.
But now, I'm older than all those greats—
older than Keats when he rolled over on tubercular bed,
older than Shelley filling lungs with last watery seconds,
older than Mayakovsky with gun to the brain, older
than Plath, Christ, I'm older than Christ—so now I know
the planet can take back its pulse at any moment.
Now I know there's no time to waste, no time to gloat
about future times, no time to go to the bar
and tell people they may not have much time.
Now I'm a  mid-career poet, whatever that means—
perhaps that I have a few books and I sit down & write—
so, here I am  writing with my eyes closed, tapping
these revered keys, imagining how long the lines grow
before I decide to hit the return. Now I'm a pro
who can sit down at the typewriter and pray for the muse
to come, but not wait on my hands till she or he arrives!
So, where are we? We are home in Astoria listening to Coltrane
in a city on alert in an era with its eyes closed shut—
we haven't been watching very closely, dear reader, have we
all these years? Nah, we can shake & bake, we can
nail 3-pointers at the last second to send the series to LA,
but what have we learned about this world when our leader
can stand on TV, unelected, mouthing 2,000-year-old clichés?
The FBI's experts all ignored their own agents' alerts
about these deranged killers, so what do they expect us to do
with such vague warnings? Hey, stop trying to scare me
and answer the friggin questions about what you should
have known & when, okay?

American people—somewhere in the tradition of Whitman,
I come not to damn but to praise, you are the spoon
of the crop, you are the pencil  at the racetrack,
you are the needle's eye that stirs the soup, you are everything
I ever asked for down at the local hardware store, you are the
purple tears in John Coltrane's horn, you are
always who you are and never who you are,
you are a big peoples, you are the wind that circles
around my neck, you are a vegetarian's choice of desserts,

you are all things to no one, everything to a few, you
laugh like a quasar galloping across the universe,
you sneak through your secret compartment unnoticed,
you trip onto the balcony, you are a prize-winning
dancer of klutz, you waltz to your grave in sneakers,
you are always yelling "shut up" so that you can use your
free speech, you are a cricket player who has brought
the wrong equipment to the game, your neglected haystacks
have provided a soft landing for many of my friends, you are
among the quickest the most inventive the directionless,
you are writing an unforgettable tune that no one can play, you
are a great people with truckloads of kindness rolling
just below the surface of your highways, and veterans
or not, I love almost every single one of you, I will keep
doing the best I can to write one more poem before I die.

2002

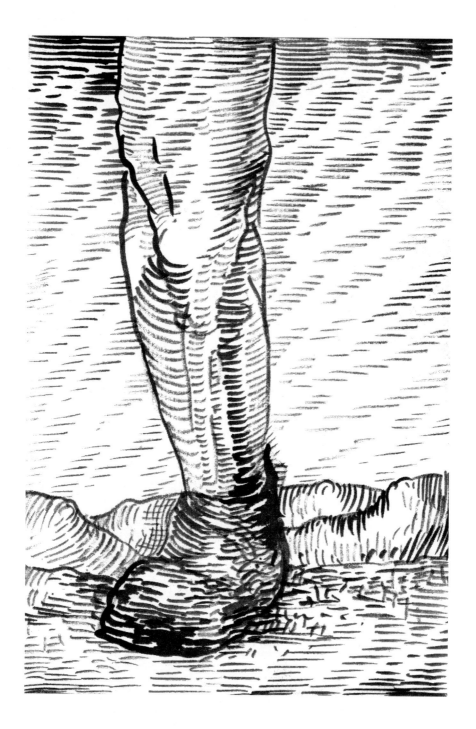

# The Knowledge Gap

While death is the most unknown element of life
        there's plenty of other shit
        we may never understand
Take Yucca Mountain, and its future piles of plutonium
        that will either lie there still, or slither
        into groundwater a half million years
Take the nuclear standoff between India and Pakistan
        Why is it that the human ego so often
        refuses to budge when best
Why is it the earth turns on its axis without ever
        knocking sense into our leaders
        or into our ability to elect them
It's lack of knowledge, more than death, that's the source of tragedy
        we grow desperate wondering what would happen
        if our internal quarks become unglued
We weep not knowing why equations give us dimensions
        of space we can never be sure exist
        tunnels within tunnels to feed our imaginations
We have no idea why the love that was once there
        has left; why the ones we cherish don't realize
        how much our presence would enhance their lives
Why those we fall in love with so often choose a more
        destructive alternative; or why exactly
        I got so lucky this time around
Of the unknown elements of life, death is the most certain
        love the most fulfilling & unpredictable
        politics the most full of human potential unrealized
Lucky for us, science continues to learn at unprecedented rates
        if we're not careful we'll erase the gap
        between life & death in no time at all
Better to be a modest nation than a lumbering giant
        walking around all day in lead boots
        and a target stamped on our forehead.

2002

# One Year Later

A year after 9/11, we still inhale the dust of our dead —
　　　　still read *NY Times* portraits of a Springsteen fan,
　　　　　　　　a lasagna home-cooking specialist, a woman
who would do anything for family & friends —
　　　　we still mourn our losses one by one,
　　　　　　　　as it should be, here & everywhere.
Yet expressing low-level radioactive concern for innocent deaths
　　　　outside America has brought atomic rebuke
　　　　　　　　in cosmopolitan circles larger than expected:
When those towering guardians of our skyline psyches collapsed
　　　　and 3,000 innocent and experienced souls were crushed,
　　　　　　　　I dove deep into the blue mourning pool
with empathetic swimmers all across America,
　　　　still trying to keep a backstroke going, balanced
　　　　　　　　between a weightless hope & a sprint of despair.
But no matter what they say on those 24/7 right-wing talk shows,
　　　　I just don't think we honor our dead
　　　　　　　　by inventing new generations of mini-nukes
& thermobaric bombs to suck the air from caves, launching
　　　　a prime-number series of pre-emptive wars
　　　　　　　　beginning with Iraq,
designing carnavoric computer programs to chew up private letters,
　　　　or registering a million roving urban snitches to spy
　　　　　　　　on neighbors from Orwellian TV repair trucks.
Is it blasphemous now to advocate new foreign policies
　　　　condemning bloodsoaked terror across the board,
　　　　　　　　curing the plague of weapons sales across the globe,
ending Cold War-born hypocrisies that describe "our" terrorists
　　　　as freedom fighters, "our" deathsquad dictatorships
　　　　　　　　as fledgling democracies?
We who call for more democratic & humane foreign policies
　　　　to make America more loved and just
　　　　　　　　are not blaming this beautiful land & people
for a mass murder unjustifiable, just including America in
　　　　with the rest of the species, full of generous medicinal spirits
　　　　　　　　and countless noble historic acts,
as well as cancerous murders almost too painful to recall.
　　　　Isn't extending the generous and the noble
　　　　　　　　still one acceptable way to honor our dead?

　　　　　　　　　　　　　Sept. 2002

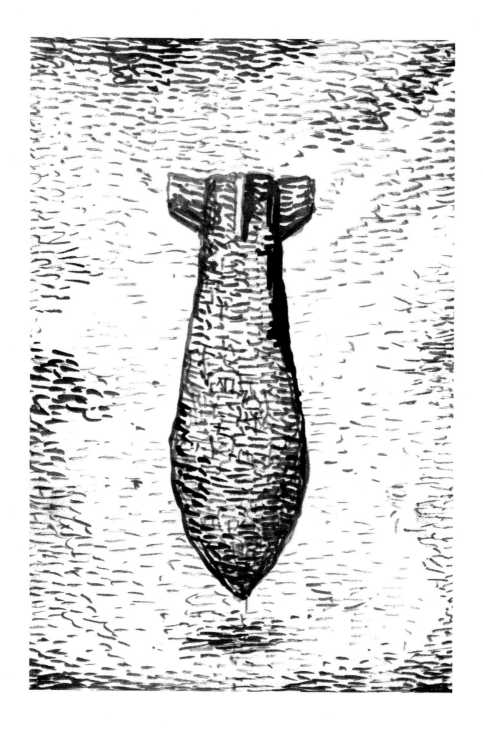

# Can We Have Some Peace and Quiet Please?

The belligerent voices are yelling in the streets
& on the radios calling for the big bombs of peace
to fall, the smart bombs, the bombs that have passed
their college entrance exams. It's Orwellian the way
everyone claims Orwell for their side—these days
everyone is fighting on behalf of Orwell and God.
Years ago Don Rumsfeld & Saddam Hussein met in
the corner & exchanged secret diplomatic handshakes—
it is only after peaceful gestures like these that the missiles
can fly. In the meantime, the time between the world
mean as is and the world we mean to become,
the endless rains are Yehuda Amichai's tears watching men
still violently beating their swords into plowshares and back
into rifles & remote-control fighter planes. On the corner
of Spring & Broadway, a taxicab driver threw a baby lamb
out the passenger-side window—everyone in a two-block radius
ran away screaming. In New York City the yelling is
so loud and the quiet so quiet that everyone I know, just below
the surface, is scared out their wits, knowing the violence
these days that can follow an apparent peace. They are calling
Senators with empathetic American voices, urging earthly
generosity and kindness, which the corporate media & our
elected leaders interpret as a vote for pre-emptive strikes.
The next century's gods have not yet been born and the last
century's are no longer able to show a child the simple
magic trick of pulling its fingers away from a newly lit flame.

2002

# A Day in the Elephant Park

Bush's spokesman Ari Fleischer tells the world press that nobody
but nobody wants to avoid war more than President Bush.
We are sleeping in a park, being run over by hundreds of giraffes—
occasionally a stray elephant smashes our foreheads into the
wet ground. We feel lucky to be alive, but we think the new massage
toys are a little too rough. We are trying to use paper cups
to hold back the waterfall of war. When we wake up under
the overbearing sun, there are Parisian vultures circling overhead.
These are the old softy vultures, the new more courageous vultures
are on their way flying from former Soviet republics where leaders
have time to shake our administration's hands in between show trials
and contemporary confessions. The giraffes have long necks, they are
beautiful. There are bombs that put on the most dazzling light shows
any of us have ever seen. We have our TVs tuned to CNN, to Fox
News, to MSNBC, we know that a lively presentation of
Independence Day fireworks is due to surprise us any week now.
Have you ever seen how much water those elephant trunks can
hold? It's a miracle of nature—God is definitely on the side of these
mythic mammals and rough sex toys. In the White House they are
mouthing a lipservice mantra against war, but sending in a few hundred
thousand troops just in case. In a few weeks, it will be considered
irresponsible and dangerous to keep those troops in the desert
without letting them loose for at least a moderately heartpounding
calisthenics routine. At first, the claim was that Saddam would never
let UN inspectors have unfettered access, now it is the lack
of evidence that proves the evidence exists. The goalposts have
moved, so the UN can be bribed or disregarded, though Saddam's
disrespect for the UN is cited as the main excuse for war. I think
Bush & Co. have an understandable paranoia—after all, Saddam
is a tyrannical former U.S. ally with reason to want revenge—
but even honest paranoia isn't a convincing rationale for bombing
the people one is pretending to save, or for declaring bankruptcy
of the imagination by declaring the immoral precedent of preventive
war. So, instead, a thousand possible reasons are placed into a
digital mixing bowl and it is you, my friend, who will pick the last
excuse on the back of a raspberry-flavored playing card. Colin
Powell says that if Saddam uses biological or chemical weapons
the U.S. just might use nuclear bombs to prevent a holocaust.
Even the giraffes and elephants stumble around the park trying
to figure that one out. Whether we are able to get a good night's sleep
or not, the smart bombs are in the back room packing; if you'd like
to know what underwear they're wearing, stay tuned to CNN at ten.

Jan. 2003

## Playing Catch with a Cracked Globe

The first thing to remember is bend at the knees & keep yr back
relatively straight.
It could be a long day filled with leapfrogging pitfalls—
easy to throw out spinal discs or lose a wig in the wind.
Most important is learning the two-arms-underneath technique:
Let the globe come to you, breathe in slowly, feel torso expand,
follow yr breath out yr nostrils, winding its calm way through
the wintry universe.
Visualize a cracked globe landing softly in your cupped palms
and whatever else you do, don't squeeze! Or shards will fly!
Anonymous millions have had throats slashed, parliaments
dissolved,
for such frivolous crimes as a too-tight grip, or turning
prematurely away.

How throw the globe back to its sender depends on its age.
If the globe's from 1492, it is likely the oldest in existence.
If necessary, wait frozen & careful all night in a half-throwing
position—
it's your butt on the line any time either of you, sender or catcher,
drops this ball.
Stare closely like a kabbalist at the letters on yr globe & it will
slowly reveal its codes—
in what ways is your globe already out of date & yet also
a compass for the future?
How does its cartography construct the world as well as
reproduce it?
Who agreed to draw its national borders in solid black marker
rather than dotted gray lines?
What political features has the author left out by paying such
close attention to proportion and typography?
Is this a Wolves of War globe, or a mapping of peaceful
emigration routes?
Who decided to include those beautiful & hideous flags?
What company funded the making of this globe anyway?

Have your masking tape ready, your crazy glue, your double
lines of epoxy,
steady your lavender candle to drip hot wax to cover the
smallest, freshest cracks.
Trace the open space from its ruptured beginning to end.
See if it passes through a country called East Timor, Zaire,
Panama, USSR.
See if the East and West of Germany are divided, the North

& South of Vietnam.
Does the globe say Israel and Palestine yet? How many
          separate nations lie within the former Yugoslavia?
How does your globe assign responsibility for Africa's wars?
Shake yr globe a little to see if there are any secret prizes inside.

Feel the surface of the U.S.A.: Can you sense the gorgeous
          Great Lakes, the magnificent Mississippi,
the majestic Rocky Mountains, the Grand Canyon wonder
          of the world?
Can you feel the dangerous radioactivity emanating from land
          lined with plutonium hair triggers?
If yr globe was made during the new millennium it will be difficult
          to locate origins of the crack.
There are Al Qaeda volcanos capable of causing leaks anywhere.
There are Colombian army earthquakes, Chechnyan firestorms,
          religious wars baking in the Kashmirian sun,
burial grounds housing too many bodies in the Congolese streets,
AIDS spreading alarming rates in every nation with populations
          indexed on the map.
There is a mountain below the Equator called IMF, a WTO River
          whose tributaries remain invisible.
There are oil tankers crossing oceans with unknown corporate logos,
tribal warlords and paramilitary death squads, homelessness
          & bone-thinning poverty.
The weather become too warm, the weapons too destructive
          and too many.
There are random subatomic pin pricks capable of carnage
          neither physics nor geography can fully explain.

Your odds of returning a new globe safely shd improve
          if you put your right palm on South America,
but no matter what method is used, in truth there is no
          foolproof way to send back a cracked globe
without risking it smashing to bits. But you have made the tough
          catch & must do something.
It will be difficult to invent a new way of throwing —
in times like these, the imagination is worth more than
          a thousand pair of hands.

                              2003

## Astoria Dream

A few weeks ago Vivian passed
her American citizenship test.
In my dream last night
I was testing her to become
a citizen of Queens.
What was the name, I asked,
of the third album by The Ramones?
When I woke up, I realized
I wasn't yet a citizen of Queens either.

2003

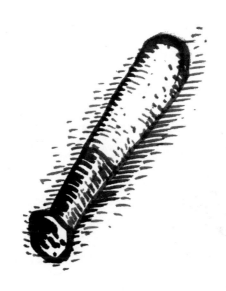

## 31st Street

On 31st Street, Astoria,
I ran into an old woman
who'd lost love ones
            in 17 wars.
"How do you smile?" I asked her.
"My shoes are too tight,"
            she answered.
"I think if I keep walking
            one day they'll stretch."


                        2003

# Shock TV, Day One

After a night of embedded TV reporters
      riding atop U.S. military trucks
            & modeling ziptight chemical jumpsuits
after a slow night of videotaped tank races
      running Iraqi deserts toward Basra & Baghdad
            a mid-east version of the televised OJ chase
a night of illusion making it seem this would be an easy war
      requiring little of the bombing
            that had been threatened & feared
today the "shock and awe" operation was launched
      and was truly shocking
            watching fireworks & shooting stars
moving thru Iraqi night skies
      watching smoke & mushroom-shaped fires rising
            o'er the city's ancient skyline
but not a single report or picture showing effects
      on city's 5 million residents or asking whether
            this sort of unsanctioned awe is illegal terror.

On ABC News, a young reporter named Richard Engel
      is perched atop Palestine Hotel's 14th floor
            his personal shock evident: "I am watching
half of Baghdad being destroyed" as 300+ cruise missiles
      fly into buildings a few miles away
            Pentagon has confirmed this is "A-Day"
Engel is stunned and stumbling, he has never seen
      anything like this before, he hopes his colleagues
            in the Al Rashid hotel across Tigris River okay
Peter Jennings back home assures him generals
      say 90% of missiles falling are smart bombs
            & Engels in a line of journalistic poesy
expresses hope the other 10% are a bit clever as well
      Jennings once again reassures the Pentagon
            is committed to keeping this modern city intact
even though the dropping of cruise missiles & bunker bombs
      the burning of offices & archaeological ruins
            is a strange way to create urban glue.

Peter Arnett, vilified twelve years earlier
      for reporting Gulf War I on CNN from Baghdad
            is back in town working for NBC
Watching the fireworks of Gulf War II, Arnett notes
      this is bigger than the last one
            "they are taking out whole buildings

with these explosions." Arnett estimates 25 buildings
                have been destroyed in last 10 minutes
                            I wonder whether these buildings waited
for civilians & young draftees to leave before exploding in flames
                before they crumbled to ground
                            crushing their inhabitants
After the WTC, isn't this kind of attack even the least bit
                worrisome to America's press—can we hear
                            what concerned New Yorkers are saying?


CNN stays with pictures of Baghdad smoldering
                in flames and rolling black smoke
                            Would it be possible to turn cameras
to the ground and see whether any bodies are visible
                running from falling ash and leaping heat
                            or perhaps lying peacefully in the street
We are told operating electricity and open phone lines are signs
                of U.S. accuracy—so doesn't anyone on CNN have the number
                            of an Iraqi family or peace witness to dial up
When a new bomb falls, Wolf Blitzer indeed seems awed
                "Look at that explosion!"  Even on right-wing Fox News
                            a young correspondent in Baghad is unnerved
says he felt shock waves running across Tigris River
                to where he's standing. He has counted
                            about 30 missiles fallen
As his phone line is going dead, the guy notes
                he has no reason to believe his situation is
                            worse than _____
an unfinished, postmodern line just waiting for viewers
                to fill in the blank—what do you think dear viewer
                            about this beautiful spring day of shock and awe?


Flipping channels, I notice one reporter get carried away
                saying the pictures & explosions from Baghdad
                            "really did look like Dresden"
a comment which Donald Rumsfeld apparently saw as well
                and disputed during his press conference, noting
                            the vast difference between dumb & educated bombs
According to Rumsfeld, carried in the opposite direction
                the hundreds of cruise missiles dropped this afternoon
                            exhibited "the humanity that goes into the targeting"
The mass bombing and depleted uranium-tipped missiles
                are thus part of a "humane effort" that was begun
                            after every single other option had been tried
Why do American reporters accept Pentagon war logic
                that once battles have begun

it is too late to ask root questions any longer
Why doesn't a single American reporter ask when such options
as these were tried: flood of human rights observers,
continued inspections, the endless nonwar imagination
following UN-sanctioned international law to maintain moral
& practical precedent on this ever-shifting Earth
Will the tough questions be arriving any time soon?

The president's spokesman Ari Fleischer holds his own conference
and claims our unelected president regrets Saddam
has put innocent people in harm's way
Ari asserts "use of force is being used to help settle this
in the most peaceful way possible"
& not a single reporter vocalizes the obvious
though crowd does express surprise Bush doesn't care
enough about their daily work or war's damage
to bother watching televised pictures this historic day
Flipping channels, a young pilot returning to his ship
from first bombing mission
reports it was "really neat"
and a "heck of an experience" that he wasn't sure
he would ever have chance to enact
after consigned to TV watching Gulf War I.
Wall Street apparently agrees that shock & awe was neat—
market up 230 points! Anything, even death & destruction,
is better than uncertainty for investor confidence!

On CBS News, Dan Rather notes we are seeing war
"with its million horrors, as Shelley once wrote"
and it is nice to see a poet in day's linguistic mix
Rather observes Baghdad is burning,
"but only in specific places" as if
that would offer total comfort in NY or Chicago
On NBC, Tom Brokaw interviews mother
of a U.S. Marine early casualty
Before she says goodbye
she wants to make a point about television coverage
the technology that brings war to the nation
brings 24-hour anxiety to parents & families
Brokaw nods sympathetically, promising to remind viewers
more often that war is not about technology
but real human lives
and in another moment we are back to flashes and fires
and pops and smokes and tank treads and rationalizations
of former generals and right-wing hacks.

This is a war whose core legality & morality hasn't been questioned
by a single US reporter all day any channel— they are wearing
Pentagon's label "Operation Iraqi Freedom"
and half day later still no investigations on American TV
into civilian casualties on "A-Day"
"a spectacular light show"
We will have to check internet next few days
www.iraqbodycount.net to find inquisitive reporters
who bother to dig into such questions
At 7:30 New York time, CNN notes there are still
a few more hours of darkness in Iraq
for bombs of shock and awe to drop
What if this entire war, no matter how quickly it ends
no matter whether those bombs pass their IQ tests
no matter whether only a few
western working-class troops are lost, no matter whether Iraqis
who do not lose family & friends eventually greet
American troops with dancing yellow roses
what if nonetheless this war was a callous gamble with human lives
launched in violation of international law & ethical ties
how hold our leaders & "free press" accountable
Perhaps the antiwar movement growing daily in creativity & size
can sprinkle some visionary seeds & long-term strategies
how choose a better one, of other worlds still possible?

Eliot Katz
3/03

# Marching for Our Own Protection

On the second day of shock and awe
        there are a quarter million people
            marching down Broadway
from Times Square to Washington Square Park.
        The signs are a tapestry of utopian hope
           & humor & reassurance
to the world there are millions of sane
        Americans who do not think
           killing a good idea
who did not vote for Cruise Missiles and uranium-tipped
        bunker bombs. Sure, we support our troops
           and want them brought home now,
but we are also concerned for Iraqi civilians
        caught in the cross-hairs of strange satellites
           and politicians who have lost
their minds. While right-wing talking heads call
        for national unity and the sometimes-opposition
           party in Congress relents,
it is American citizens keeping our nation safe
        by showing that humanity yet lives
           in this country of weapons & dreams.

March 20, 2003

# The Cakewalk

The cakewalk
has become a bit sticky

some Iraqis have turned
their daisies

into rifles
& hand grenades

seems many
don't like tyrant Saddam

nor foreign invaders
dropping cruise missiles

and cluster bombs
In Basra the water supply

has been cut off
and we are seeing

the possibility
of humanitarian disaster

war should never
have been viewed

as a latenight poker game
initiated by those

too zealous
to send their own kids

into urban combat
It'll take millions of patriots

& internationalists
(truthfully the same folks)

to throw the lunatics
out the White House

Until then we are facing
more weekends from hell

as well more spring days
filled with thousands

marching down Broadway
for a democratic peace

This is one of the two
oldest stories on the planet

(both originating here)
Let the battle for ideas

replace those young corpses
growing cold under desert moons

2003

# Broken Eggshells and No Maps

They have captured Saddam in the bottom of a spider hole
unshaven & sedated, broken eggshells & poetry books
littering his lair. On the TV news networks they are
pretending that it no longer makes sense to have taken
an antiwar position, as if the capture of Saddam can
bring back 10,000 lives, can cure the broken eyesockets,
can eliminate the uranium cancer threat, can put the torn
pages back into international law books. It's a good
thing one more tyrannical leader is behind bars, but now
it's unknown whether the violence will slow or grow,
perhaps more Iraqis eager to resist the occupation
knowing the risk of Saddam climbing back on his thrown
has ceased. Or maybe the Americans will be more
widely loved, I think it's unlikely but maybe the next
elected body will request being made the 51st state? It's really
unknown, there are no maps made for this part of the new
century, the monuments are being shaped, but no one can agree
on the best material to fill the mold. Vivian, we are doing
our best to love each other in an imperfect world. If we wait
for perfection I will be 1,000 pounds heavier and the dust
from our bookcases will have long since learned to read
for itself. So we go ahead and try to improve our own
government, get one that will not suck up the healthcare,
welfare, housing, world hunger, and clean water money
into a vacuum pump of tax cuts & pulse-emitting, flesh-burning
weapons that won't work or should never be used. There is no
set formula sure to work every time. We set the temperature
to a "stop Bush" setting and then leave the room and go
to a few meetings and readings and rallies. When we return
home, we check to see whether the cake has arisen.

2003

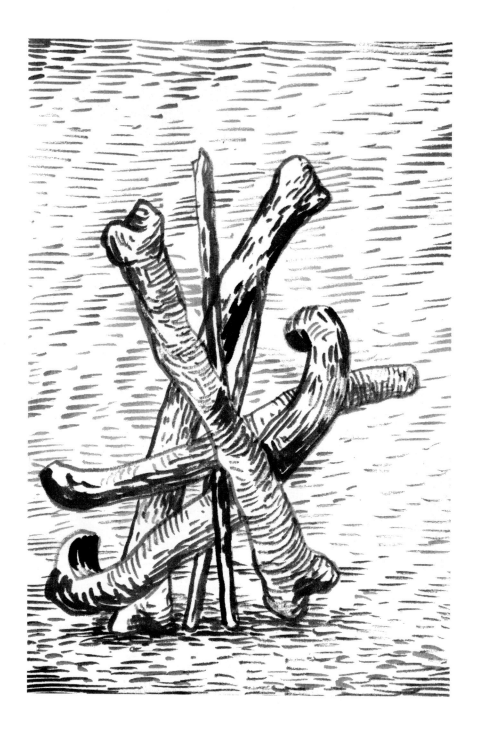

# A Half-Baked Manifesto
## for Reconstructing Broken Bones

I told the Pentagon's one-eyed guy
       this damn war'd bring thousands
              of innocent deaths & hot new recruits
into al qaeda-affiliated terror firms
       but he still lives in the Cold War & loves
              to hear the sound of young ones falling.
Now the exploding corpses in uniform & out
       are food for the birds.
              Now 200-ton nation-destroying bombs
send sacred iron pillars to break bones
       & knock down homes
              across the floating extinction of continents.
"Only acknowledge your iniquity"
       said Jeremiah in the voice of god
              but the president is coughing & scrambling
his syntax trying to explain his & his nation's
       past macrobiological mistakes.
              The Attorney General has turned
into a granite fossil while kneeling in prayer
       & compiling neon McCarthyite files
              on infants & toddlers of antiwar marchers.
Maher Arar was tortured in Syria's breadcrusted dungeon
       despite Ashcroft's assurances heard echoing
              through the background noise
of a high-speed human rights blender. Cheney still claims
       Saddam was Osama's late night lover, Rumsfeld says
              the word "Guantanamo" with the smug grin
of a man who knows it makes no difference to rusty
       corporate news anchors whether his lies
              are big or bigger. The century's most pungent
smog-filled bill is nicknamed Clear Skies Initiative,
       Healthy Forests offers loggers a free supply
              of chain saw blades. An energy reform chauffeur
drives a cab full of tax breaks to summer homes
       of those fillet-prepared to cook the globe
              over a medium flame. The national
crime prevention brigade has developed a no-fail economic
       blackmail scheme to garner flak jacket U.S. immunity
              from world's most progressive war crimes court.
Even the rose-pedaled immune systems of children
       are not immune from Bush team's sour medicine,
              where "education for all" is laconic code

for stripping schools of the last sliver of union-made paint.
Ending hunger for this shrink-wrapped administration
equals sending starved kids down
to nearest bootstrap sermon. If you ask for citizenly explanation,
their public relations spokesman
sighs it's all so undecideable
some weird kind of post-post-structuralist
vague, ungraspable reasons overflowing
horizontally across basement floor here
vertically thru 50-foot castle roof there, somebody
they are unable to identify has placed a mile-wide pothole
along the highway of American ideals.
Their made-in-Miami rubber bullet pellets
are the only justification they offer, locked & loaded
for rampaging gangs of idealistic teens.
There is no signature at bottom
of any interdepartmental forms,
no one with beating cabinet heart is available
to speak softly at the flag salute funeral, the documents
the investigative committee has requested
were shoved through the corporate paper shredder
a long time ago. There are no answers for questions
of who never knew. Who told Novak?
Who forged Niger?
How Enron money? Who slipped the 27 lies
into Bush's State of the Union speech?
Why's a Chinese semi-conductor company
paying brother Neil 2 million technophobic bucks?
How did we get from Civil Rights Act
of 1866 to here?
O that my head were waters! Lack of sleep
has become breakfast too many mornings.
The Earth has been sighing
through our open flesh wounds a quarter-million years.
The sun misses its beloved.
Our bodies self-destruct.
Our poets in the snowy cities deconstruct.
Run—the horse—cave belly ache—
corn never roots wish—
no end then beginnings—
cut wire whispering—
Which of the wanting Grand Narratives
are they talking about now? O lamentations!
O Jeremiah!  O Blake! There is no longer
a good excuse for our innocence!

142

Back in the 1980s I told the poetry world
        it was reconstruction that held the greatest
            unfulfilled emancipatory potential.
I was looking for a 14th amendment of poetry,
        a verse to reverse Plessy v. Ferguson
            for good, a new way of seeing to flip
the notion of original intent on its head, judicial doctrine
        meant to invisibly disintegrate the most utopian
            midnight desires of post-Civil War era.
Much humane good has been done in this country,
        the ideals of democracy & unimprisoned talk,
            the vote & the vatic blues,
the fight against fascism and mass migratory movements
        for peace & australopithicene-ancestored rights,
            the jazz trumpet & long lines
of bebop hiphop verse. An expanding nutritional belly
        of sometimes sustainable mirth, quantum-eyed inventions
            of some melodic medicines & humming machines.
But it is still reconstruction that is most
        in need of a 40-acre rescue. Yet I have grown
            older & occasionally smarter
& can now also say "long live
        the language poets"
            & the 10,000 other international schools,
so many diverse linguistic loves capable of digging
        up useful glory. As Nicanor Parra said,
            too much blood has been spilled
under the bridge to go on believing only one poetic
        road is right. Whether a kitchen mirror to the real,
            or Ernst Bloch's anticipatory illuminations,
Isaiah's admonition holds: "do not shed innocent
        blood in this place."
            In my most transparent moments
of realism, there is a purple horse labeled a long shot
        at the last moment reaching its neck
            across the finish line first.
In utopian fantasies I see thousands of multicolored shirts
        marching peacefully in the streets
            to throw Bolivia's president out
of the country, to send Georgia's electoral thief
        home with embarrassed eyes dangling.
            I see a new global trade organization
exporting the idea of taxfree nonviolent presidential topplings
        whichever corner of Earth they're well deserved.
            I see a Geneva-negotiated peace deal
between Israelis & Palestinians that at first offers only

a full-throated birdsong organizing tool,
but within a short time
is being implemented step by step by a less stubborn age.
I see a new president of Brazil
altering the map of incomplete bridges.
The TV Reporters of Record have tried so hard
to convince us we have no choice
but this George, too, will be dethroned.
Love, you and I will unlock our x-rayed suitcase
of buried laughter, the jobs promised
will be there for all,
no longer will any engendered group be sacrificed at altar
of an idea. Isaiah, we take the plowshares
in our broken hands.
The wound bandages itself. The burnt day care center
is rebuilt from its ashes. Our poems
have become immune to the scissors.
Reparations for slavery's non-biodegradable shackles
& native America's broken treaties will be paid.
The next plague is already cured.
Our most peaceful surrealistic phrases mean
what they say. The Human Rights Act
of 2050 is passed!

2003

## They wanted to find something they could tell the truth about

Could they tell the truth about lack of rain in Crawford, Texas
       the week he fell off his bicycle?
Could they release report of depleted-uranium cancers?
How they envision squeezing lungs of urban rent subsidies?
Could they be honest about undersea war budgets, gold
       wheelbarrows & diamond shovels, corporate highways
       leading from Bermuda to a planet still undiscovered?
What could they decide to tell the truth about?
There were no revelations possible that wouldn't endanger
       state family secrets!
Yet desire to tell a deep truth was Eating at the president's Brain!
Maybe he could tell truth about his personal demons?
The killer bees that were buzzing around his neck, searching
       for the weakness of his personal god?
Crush them! That was what he honestly felt. Surely he could
       tell the people what he intended to do with those bees.

2004

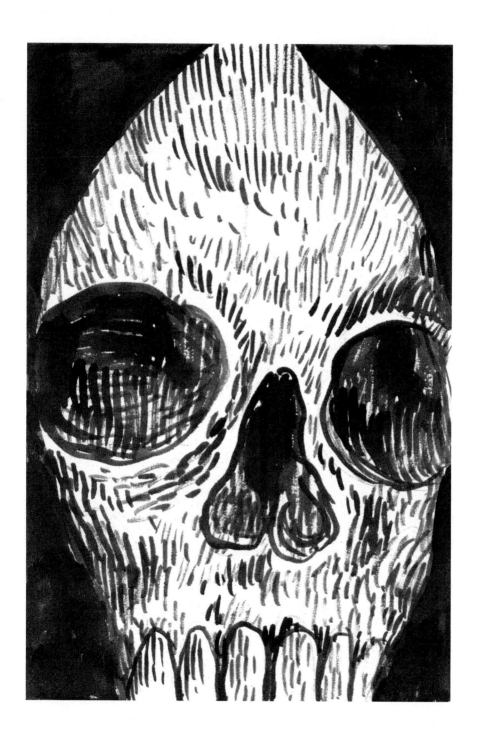

# Death and War

On the last car of a late night N train
I asked Death how it managed
        to move so quickly
                during wars.

"I'm not sure why," Death answered,
"but ever since Hiroshima
        my skates glide faster
                over the cool Earth."

I asked whether it was possible
to tell the difference
        between a civilian
                and a young draftee.

"No difference."

I said from my own perspective
there was at least something different
        about a playful child
                struck by stray cluster bomb.

Death glared between my eyes.

I debated with Death about the merits
of a bullet, a car crash, & a baseball bat—
        It confessed the first case
                of pediatric AIDS

had almost bounced back & shocked Death
        to death.

Approaching the last stop, I asked
whether it ever thought,
        despite a difficult economy,
                to look for an easier job.

Death laughed & pointed to the front page
of today's *New York Times*:
        "Watch your step, E. Katz,
                but don't make it obvious."

2004

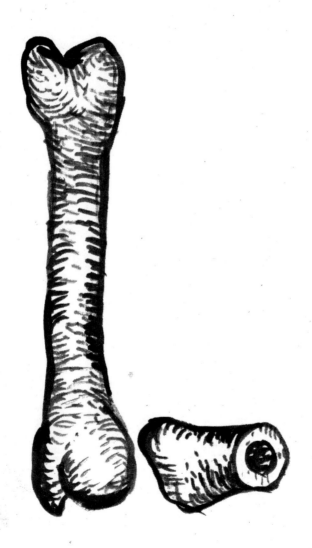

# On looking at a Leon Golub print

Like the best prophetic artists he gave a body
to human error, a body both real as a rifle & alive
as a dream. Leon was one of those generous souls
who insisted we view our own demonic creations
up close. The first exhibit of his I saw was in lobby
of Brooklyn Museum. He'd photocopied his giant
canvasses of post-1960's American-led halls of horror—
Vietnam, Central America, Southern Africa—
onto life-sized transparencies hung loosely from ceiling
& swaying calmly in open-door New York City
breeze. When looking at an individual piece, one
couldn't help but see gun-butt, iron-boot torture
with American pedestrians strolling nonchalantly behind
the scene, going casually dressed lives as our leaders
bankrolled foreign bullies with exploding helicopter dollars
& giftwrapped prisons stuffed full of our country's
two-plus centuries of uncivil liberty's rarely free press.
A few years earlier, as a Golub fan from seeing his work
in books, I'd written out of the blue, a poet-stranger
asking whether he might consider donating a drawing
for front cover of my first book. In thinking of artists
whose work I'd admired from afar, I figured I'd take
longest shot first. Leon was teaching Rutgers, and I was
a New Brunswick poet & activist, so hoped he'd enjoy
references to Hub City's homeless & utopian democracy
in youthful attempts to carry on a Whitmanic tradition.
He called a few days later & invited me to visit studio
& choose among his latest 4 or 5 pieces.

About six months before he died, he told me of his cancer
over lunch, said he'd like to give me a print, that I should
call in a few weeks. Again, he laid out 4 or 5 choices
& signed one I picked. Nancy was there & I looked
at this studio, loving human interactions by a couple
who had influenced America's visual art for as long
as I'd breathed on this beautiful blue planet. This was
way we were supposed to live & grow & grow old.
This was the way we were supposed to rip away
curtains of denial & terror, take an honest look at
way blood flows up, from core of the earth until
it reaches soles of our feet, then up through night's
vibrating thighs, spotted belly, lion-hearted voice box,
to base of neck that refuses to alter its vision for sake

of the highest bidder, the skull that spends its life
building a dream to outlast the letting go of tin
& flesh. His brush was always sharp as a razor
& broad & compassionate as a velvet safety net. The print
I chose had 2-1/2 male figures shown from shoulders up,
one black, one & a half in red , with text up center
& across bottom reading: "How close can I get to Rome?
or am I kidding myself?" I am looking at that print now —
figures drawn part representational even classical, & part
modernist abstraction — & I am pondering its multiple & circular
meanings: How close can the artist get toward being
recognized among the classics? Can the black man
in picture ever hope to join the pantheon or even literally
visit the Italian city without raising unfair suspicions in times
like these? Given a white canvas background, does the full face
painted in red signify a white American, or is it a universal face
painted blood color of five centuries of America's crimes?
And what in name of Michelangelo is that half face doing,
perhaps waiting for an audience with courage or humor
able to fill in the missing parts? With brush strokes
& scraper, Leon painted the paradoxical heart of humankind
into the thread of his canvasses. What was born, built,
or bombed could all be partially erased. Fantasy is all-powerful,
but Leon still refused to leave out the fragile bones,
an artworld mix 20 years behind the times and 60 years
ahead. Staring intently at the print in our living room,
it is easy to see Leon's face within all the figures, seeds
of possibility that even brutality reveals. The eyes that saw
this world so clearly from so many different angles has now
found another. Our new century grows with a dialectical mix
of yellow cluster bombs & food can drops — with each piece
of flesh that blows away, a new seed implants in the living art.

2004

## Sitting to Praise

I am sitting down at my kitchen table
to write a praise poem
for the people of my country,
the people and the oceans—
some of the people,
and the future oceans cleansed.
I am sitting to celebrate the way Americans
have responded since 9/11
by recognizing the value of every human life,
only that's not what really happened.
But it happened for some Americans,
so I'm celebrating you—
You know who you are.

2003

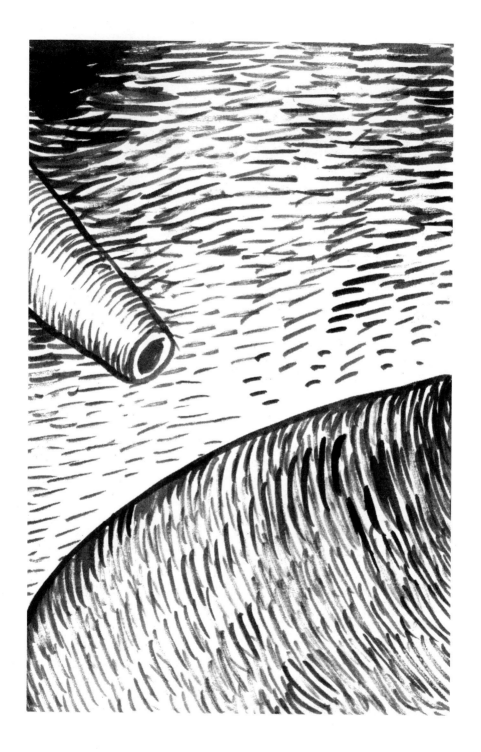

## Talking with Lord

I was in my Astoria bedroom listening to Bob Fass
        on WBAI radio, 1am,
when General Lance Lord walked in to convince me
        of the need for America to take over space.

"But space," I claimed, "cannot be owned.
As I said in a long poem years ago,
'landlord is a homosapien lie
        told to degrade the universe'."

"Son," he said, "keep spouting your poetic philosophy,
        & paying your rent."

"But once you put nukes in space, killer lasers,
        spherical gravity bombs,
you'll just as likely destroy America
        as save it."

"Son," he said, "there's a destiny that remains
        ever so slightly beyond your comprehension
You're right, though, these may just as easily kill you
        as come to your rescue."

"Why not reserve space for peaceful purposes?
        Savor our atmosphere?
As Einstein and Russell said in their manifesto
        fifty years ago,
'Remember your humanity, and forget the rest'?"

"It's impossible to walk in another man's shoes,
        or to wear another's destiny.
You, my naive friend, will never understand the need
        for nukes in space."

I was about to sadly give up protesting Lord's
        irrational obfuscations,
but realized I don't get this close to power very often
        so decided to give it one more try:

"What the fuck are you talking about!" I yelled,
        thinking extra volume might
                break through the general's denial.
"Your philosophy is gibberish, completely incoherent,

lies used as rationale to put
   our entire species at risk!
Get off your bomb-making machine!"

With my last yell, the next-door neighbor started pounding
   on our common wall,
& General Lord disappeared, leaving behind a flyer
   for next week's military ball.

2005

# From the Ground Up

To rebuild is always more difficult than to destroy
And now the people do battle with the cronies.

To stop a war on a dime takes two million acts of courage
While centrists help hold the fort like an immoveable rock.

When the rescuers are nowhere to be seen
They may be guarding their stations, armed & confused.

What this administration says can mostly be assumed a lie
And yet people find a way to make their contributions.

On the right, the passionate are talking gibberish or being indicted
On the left, we are erased from the daily news.

The displaced should have a say in New Orleans reconstruction
But the story of land taken by force predates recorded time.

More of the world's artists begin today with a blank canvass
& paint lines with invisible ink that may take years to re-appear.

2005

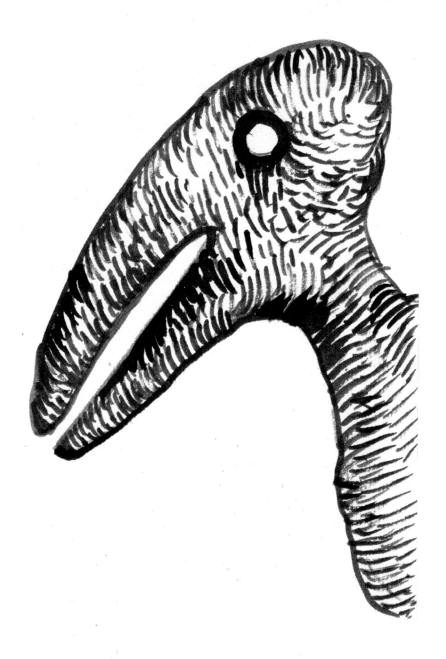

## Eve Gets Angry with God after Reading
## Her High School Science Book

On the fifth day
after the Big Bang,
God brought forth
beasts of the Earth,
including dinosaurs
all shapes and sizes.
On day six, God created
Adam & Eve, blessing
them: "be fruitful
and multiply."
Next day, God smiled
at his intelligent design
and rested.
Adam & Eve
learned quickly
to run for their lives,
trying weary best
to avoid pterodactyl's
swooping claws,
Tyrannosaurus Rex's
heart-pounding footsteps
& meat-shredding
molars, the long sharp
tusk of Triceratops.
Eve was the one
who expressed
their anger: "Why
the hell couldn't he
give evolution
a few million more years
to kill off the dinosaurs
before making us?"

2005

# Full Moon Over Falluja

Well, now we know they are lighting up the night sky with white
        phosphorus,
better able to see midnight skin melting into bone. What country is it
that would send such harsh chemical fire into a neighborhood?
In occupied territories of Palestine, a father has donated organs of his son,
killed by Israeli army, to a congregation of six, both Jewish and
Muslim. If this doesn't shame the violent of all nations into melting
their weapons, what will? Tonight, let children of earth sleep in peace
under a full moon, let skin remain the body's best organic protection,
let bones stay cool and covered—in a thousand years there will be
plenty of time for our skulls to rest in warm earth & give thanks.

2005

# Global Warming

The world reads icy newspapers
Whatever the politicians say in fine print no longer matters
It's the way the pages will yellow in the end
Finally, we've seen lava seeping through concrete walls
Finally, we've seen the rains launch upward
If thunder begins inside our own bodies, where will we hide?
They will say the question hasn't been studied enough
They will say the burning sensation is only in our imagination
They're right; and yet where does one go to escape the imagination?
To our death, that's where!
From the cemetery, the corpses no longer care what car we drive
The thigh bone in far corner prefers a Ford SUV
The skull on the left loves the roominess of a pickup truck
Even from their graves, the little ones with cancer'd spines
          are asking adults for help.

2006

# Why I Did Civil Disobedience at Wall Street with the War Resisters League

With over a half million Iraqi civilians killed as result this catastrophic war & occupation, four million others forced to flee their homes, it doesn't seem right America whoops or wails daily about consumer overconfidence second-home-sales bull-markets business-as-usual.

When I got to Wall Street holding my aching back from previous day's march, I wasn't sure whether I was well enough to join in, but an electric impulse at base of spine seemed to surge me forward & urge me sit.

A recent poll showed most Americans believe under 10,000 Iraqis have been killed—which home planet's TV reality shows are those purple patriots watching?

While America's soldiers come back homeless & wounded, Halliburton execs make millions & move their castles to Dubai—will someone please introduce a bill outlawing private contractors making more than the troops?

In his essay on civil disobedience, Thoreau said "Let your life be a counter-friction to stop the machine!"

Everyone knows the Democrats were elected to Congress to stop the war, but it seems like most of them are still wandering lost in basement halls.

I love MoveOn.org, but their calls for peace vigils only mentioned honoring dead American troops & not Iraqis buried under depleted uranium-covered earth, and I felt stronger nonviolent statement ought to be made.

Continued U.S. occupation serves as recruitment tool for extremists and as blood-boiling pot for hundreds of thousands families that've lost loved ones since 3/19/03—and all suspect rightfully Bush wants oil rights & permanent military bases!

In the police van heading to holding cells, there was great spirit of camaraderie among activists meeting first time in plastic handcuffs, coming from dozen different traditions to same stock-exchange street-corner sit-down determination.

Under current levels of chaos & destruction, seven hours in police vans and holding cells seemed like small form of existential penance an American could pay on 4th anniversary of the war.

2007

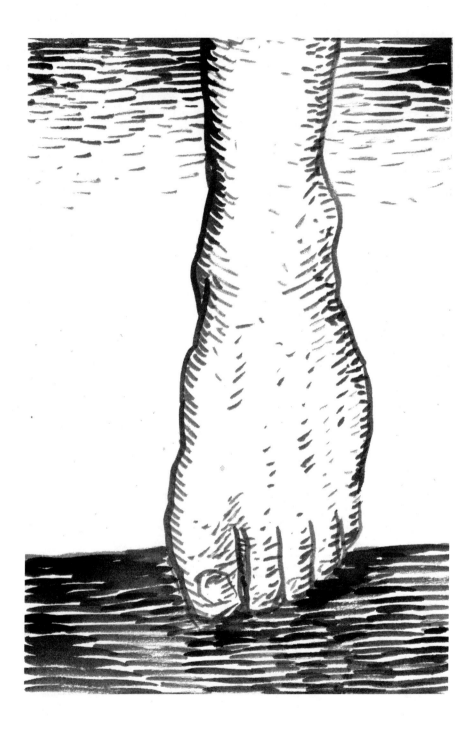

# Marching Barefoot

By the tens of thousands, Burmese Buddhist monks are shown
on blogger videos marching bravely and barefoot
for democracy and a decent economic life. America's president
knows that childrens are learning, so he speaks to the U.N.
with a cue-card of mispronunciations in his cupped palm, making
declarations about the Universal Declaration of Human Rights
that come without a shred of credibility attached. Which
country will lose the race to recognize the human rights
to housing and health care? These are perilous times
for pedestrians walking in bare feet. Too many leaders East West
North and South have refused to sign the treaty to keep
used razor blades off their city sidewalks. Where ever we take
a stroll these days we are stepping on globalized blood.

2007

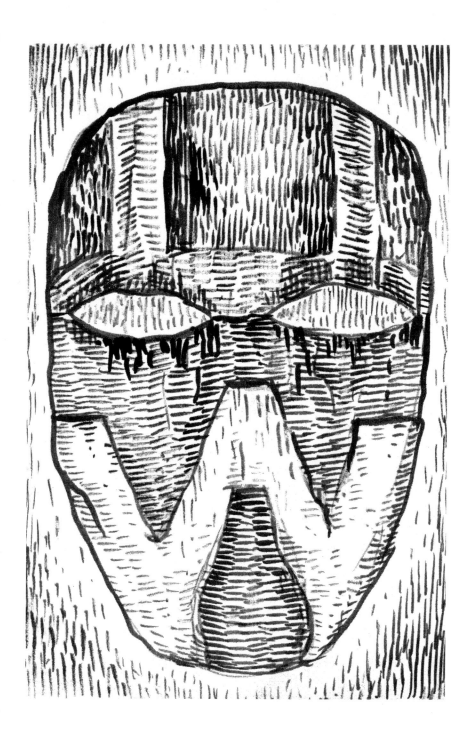

# We Are Trying to Change

Twenty percent of Iraq is dead or fled
and the moon over the Pentagon is purple

with glee. The war mask is on
& Congress has decided not

to de-fang it. There are desert valleys
and polluted streams all across the planet,

but the flames in Iraq have grown hotter
than the sparks in an old Albanian kitchen—

and this is a fire that we have seen
people we once knew light. So we spend

five nights each week doing our best
to extinguish. On nights six and seven,

we get no rest, but must place our minds
onto a different set of bedpost spikes.

A new British study says 1.2 million
civilians have died, a figure so stunning

it barely gets reported. Bad knees
and all, we are walking in the streets

hoping to help arrest our president. The city's
police think we are their private comedy club,

but at least we are rushing the stage
& trying to change the color of the moon.

2007

# Unlocking the Language Room of War

*(A Talk Given at Fairness & Accuracy in Reporting's "March on the Media,"*
*Republican Convention Protests, NYC)*

The late poet Allen Ginsberg, who was a teacher and friend, knew that issues of media and language were crucial to our prospects for building a real and humane democracy in America. Allen was an avid reader of the alternative press, and an enthusiastic supporter of the group, Fairness and Accuracy in Reporting. In one of his great antiwar poems of the Vietnam era, "Wichita Vortex Sutra," Allen challenged the "amnesia" and "television language" of the corporate media and wrote: "I search for the language / that is also yours / almost all our language has been taxed by war." How relevant those words sound today.

Later in the same poem, Allen called all "Powers of imagination" to his side and wrote the memorable line, "I here declare the end of the War!" Allen's idea was that, in the poet-prophet tradition, what can be imagined can one day be made real.

Unfortunately, it is rare to find anything close to that level of imagination in our mainstream media, which these last few years has all-too-often seemed locked in the language of war.

Locked in the language of war, it's impossible to find another way out.

Locked in the language of war, the corporate media too often locked out sensible antiwar voices, failed to tell the public often enough that there was no connection between Saddam Hussein and 9/11, and failed to highlight strongly enough that weapons inspectors before the war had followed U.S. intelligence agency leads and had not found any WMD's.

Locked in the language of war, the mainstream press was unable to untangle the adminstration's knotted and contradictory prewar justifications, just as it has been unable to highlight and explore the recent Freudian revelations of President Bush saying that Iraq has been a "catastrophic success" and that his administration is constantly looking for new ways to harm our country.

Locked in the language of war, no mainstream media outlet has devoted sufficient attention to the question of how many Iraqis have been killed or seriously injured in this unnecessary adventure.

Locked in the language of war, the mainstream media failed to explore alternative ways that solidarity might have been expressed with the Iraqi people without bombing and maiming the people the neocons were claiming to want to liberate.

Inside the language of war, we continue to get sound-bite explanations and historical amnesia.

Locked in the language of war, the major media failed to point out that the Bush administration was effectively declaring bankruptcy of the imagination by undertaking the illegal and immoral precedent of preventive war.

Locked and lost in the language of war, the corporate media's half-hearted apologies for their pre-war coverage inevitably come too late and not nearly deep enough.

Look at the magnifying lens through which the media has tried to find any tiny instance of violence on the part of those of us protesting the Bush agenda here in NYC this week. What if that lens was used instead to look at the death and destruction caused by war? Why isn't that magnifying lens, for example, used to look at the dangers of depleted uranium weapons, which were used so widely in this Iraq war and which seem to have been causing cancer and birth defects in Iraqi civilians as well as American troops since their use in the first Gulf War. After this week of news coverage, I've come to think that in order to get the mainstream press to focus more closely on whether Depleted Uranium ought to be banned as a weapon of widespread destruction, we would need to announce that the DU missiles are lining up for a peace march and that some of them are anarchists.

Of course, it's not only in the area of foreign policy that our mainstream press shows its lack of imagination. Night after endless TV night, the networks cite changes in the stock exchange as an implied indicator of the state of the American economy, an indicator that sometimes seems to lodge in the subconscious even of Americans who don't own much or any stock. Instead of, or in addition to, stock exchange numbers, imagine what would happen if CBS ABC CNN FOX MSNBC gave us nightly figures for the increasing number of homeless people in America, whether the number of those going without health insurance is up or down, whether more or fewer people around the world have access to clean water tonight? With such daily scorekeeping, wouldn't our elected leaders be more likely to find the resources to address these urgent social needs?

Too often these days, led by Fox, cable TV news seems to news what professional wrestling is to wrestling. There may be nuggets of genuine news and analysis in there somewhere, but those nuggets can be difficult to find beneath the hype, the bluster, the pre-scripted storylines, and the limited scope of so-called experts and ideas. Professional wrestling may get good ratings, but that doesn't make it honest. And that doesn't mean it provides the information on which a thriving democracy depends.

While we work to challenge and improve the mainstream media, it is lucky for the planet that we have the fast-growing independent media; that we have inventive writers and artists envisioning and sketching more humane possibilities that might one day be made real; and that we have millions of creative citizens of the world, many of whom have come to rally in NYC during the Republican convention to expose the harmful and unjust policies of the Bush administration, to "press the press" as my friend Danny Schechter the News Dissector puts it, and to unlock the doors that hold the language of war in place and speak out in myriad ways to move our country in a new direction—one that reflects our most progressive democratic, egalitarian, peaceful, and ecological principles.

2004

# Coda

# Poems on Other Planets with Intelligent Life

## Planet 75

It was a windy day in Northern Alberta. Who knows what it was like in New York City? In New York, everyone believes they're at the center of the universe. Around the universe, many have read stories about the crash in Roswell, New Mexico, but very few have even heard of New York. Out on Planet 75, the Big Apple is three hundred feet tall and tasty as chocolate.

## Planet 76

From Planet 76, the ten moons look like they change colors every three nights. But it's really the inhabitants' eyeballs that all undergo color-spectrum transformation in sync. The eyeball change results from eating rare fruit delicacies grown in the coldest freezer in the Twelve Galaxies. If an earthling ever tried to eat this fruit, his or her eyeballs would leave their sockets and travel the bloodstream straight to the feet.

## Planet 77

America will hopefully soon have its first black president, Barack Obama. On Planet 77, they are watching the U.S. election sitting on pins and needles. Literally. Ever since Planet 77 elected their first striped president, the world's chairs have mostly been outfitted with do-it-yourself acupuncture equipment. The beings of Planet 77 like Barack Obama, but they think his health care proposal is much too timid.

## Planet 78

It takes a village of nineteen to produce a child on Planet 78. If just one being puts its thing-a-ma-bob in the wrong thing-a-ma-socket, the resulting kid will walk backwards for the rest of its life. That could be as many as 500,000 earth years. After a normal birth, ten of the nineteen raise the child as parents; the other nine look for another half-village to thing-a-ma-bob.

## Planet 79

The life forms are so way out on Planet 79 that the closest resemblance on Earth is a helium balloon, tugged and twisted like comedian Steve Martin's early balloon-animal skits. After 240 revolutions around the planet's sun, the air in each being exhausts itself and the creature collapses to the ground and expires. Until this horrible death, these creatures have a blast, criss-crossing their brown skies and blue mountains. "Who's up high today?" Rirek greets Kadir as they fly into each other and try their best not to pop.

## Planet 80

No such thing as parenthood here, the children wouldn't tolerate it. Neuroses were passed down from too many generations until a majority of babes decided to just say no. At age two, the infants begin crawling along and calling out the names of their teachers. If a teacher does a bad job, some children on Planet 80 will send that teacher to a punishment that no language on Earth is capable of describing.

## Planet 81

The corn on Planet 81 talks until it's plucked from its stalk to be eaten. Right before Jayjay went out to the field for her breakfast, one corn shouted in his ear, "murderer"! Until then, no corn on the planet had ever rebelled. Jayjay left the dissident corn on its stalk and went home to design a corn muzzle.

## Planet 82

Each generation had invented a more lethal laser beam than the last. When the current generation figured out how to mount its guns aboard flying saucers, entire portions of Planet 82 were disintegrated. Huge populations on the ground agreed to work cheaply for the laser-bearing pilots in flying discs. One day a half-dozen workers wandered by accident into a waste dump and noticed a previous era's ray guns that had been tossed in the trash. A few of the guns that had been discarded still worked, but the flying saucers were too quick for this old-school technology, and the pilots ruthlessly incinerated the entire country from where these shots were fired. Workers in other countries started secretly building underground science labs, spending their nights trying to invent speedy trains made of mirrors that might deflect the laser beams and improve their bargaining position.

## Planet 83

The daily winds would drive any human over the cliff, but somehow the organisms on Planet 83 are able to dig in and live a semi-normal life. They don't move much, though, maybe a few hundred meters over a thousand year average life. To compensate for lack of travel, home life is like another world. The beds the most inviting in the universe. Sex lives like beings on 99% of the planets will never experience.

## Planet 84

After a million years of evolution, there's no need to eat. Breathing in the nutrition-enhanced atmosphere satisfies the food needs of every living thing on Planet 84. Amazing the extra leisure time afforded by never having to hunt, gather, buy, or prepare meals. No worries here about the kids going to sleep hungry. For some reason, though, the digestive systems go through all the regular motions, with toilets big enough to fill two-thirds of every home.

*Planet 85*

The rulers of Country #62 on Planet #85 are obsessed with the system of imprisonment and torture in Uzbekistan. They've studied Zimbabwe, Burma, Colombia, and Guantanamo Bay, but for some reason they ended up fixated on the idea of boiling prisoners alive. They don't even look for answers anymore, just get right to the torture method they believe is the most sensational ever devised. The problem is there's very little water on Planet 85, and more and more of it is being used for torture. The rulers of Country #62 are planning in 20 years to fly down and take over Uzbekistan to suck up the water and bring it home.

June 2008

# Grounding the Nerves

Feeling mostly grounded on Nose mountaintop, eighth summer visiting,
  sitting near Vivian's calm breath with forest million acres view
  out side window.
This year, I'm having weird feet problems, numbness or pins and needles
  in both feet each time I sit for even a few minutes.
My New York doctor took a too-quick look few days ago and said he
  thinks my blood circulation is fine, probably a slightly pinched
  nerve emanating from chronic spine problems.
Well, I've lived with at least a little back pain every day for twenty years,
  what's another few decades?
Even if I don't have another few decades, it's been mostly a good 51 years
  filled with electric poems and friends, a full life offering one more
  set of hands to help put world's jigsaw puzzle pieces together in a
  shape that comes a little closer to a comfortable fit.
When I left the States, all Cable TV political talk was examining Obama
  and McCain's latest flip-flops, Obama foregoing public financing
  now that he realizes he can raise sound-barrier-breaking millions
  online,
McCain supporting offshore oil drilling to shore up slippery corporate
  fundraising base and make awkward seductive pitch for those
  worried drivers riding razor's edge because of rising gas prices
  and the housing economic floorboard bubble pop.
Despite his flip-flops, McCain is a closed book—we know in advance he's
  going to govern as right-wingéd hawk, even if some in media still
  look into his eyes and see a cuddly pet dog maverick.
Obama is an open window, not enough information to predict with
  certainty whether he'll preside as centrist campaigner he's been or
  remain more receptive than Bill Clinton was to grassroots
  movement pressure that could remind him of a human rights-
  brimming community organizer past.
He seems like a good guy & did take good position praising Supreme
  Court's decision that Guantanamo detainees have fundamental
  habeas corpus rights despite polls showing that an unpopular
  opinion in an America where too many remain hoodwinked by
  Bush's legacy of Presidential Fright.
If Obama wins, which I hope he will, an important historic first, let's keep
  the pressure on; it'll take some mountainous detours from the
  current presidential path to put America's circulation and
  nervous systems in order.


June 2008

# Bail Out What?

As the U.S.-built trojan-horse mortgage-backed insecurities
crisis continues to hop aboard freight elevators moving
continually downwards; as the Wall Street bull let loose from its
iron base continues to rampage through the trickle-down
bloody back streets of overworked America; as a discredited
treasury department of a disgraced presidency attempts to tickle
nation's plastic-card wallets by yet one more midnight
pour-oil-down-the-bank-chimney approach; as Congress shrugs
its confused shoulders and nods in sleepy assent, with Democrats
making sure recruit enough Republican votes to share blame
for a firecracker bill they all knew in advance was a dud; as nervous
homeowners and shopkeepers wait by silent phones for a sign
from heaven that manna-tasting loans and credit cards are
raining from the skies in infinite variety of shapes and sizes;
as the four corners of the decade's deregulated pyramid
scheme prove no match for international capital's globalized
wrecking ball; why should it surprise that a chef's knife can't carve
edible food out of a stack of blowing thousand-dollar bills?

With all major commentators warning about the need to halt
the next Great Depression, where's the proposal for a new
New Deal? Why not Dems voting for bills they are proud
to pass alone, and then watch Bush sign because embarrassed
there is no other rational or irrational choice? Why not put world's
heaviest military budget on a strict low-carb diet? Why not new
olive-green bridge-building projects paying a guaranteed living wage?
Why not freeze foreclosures and send $10,000 checks to every
struggling renter and homeless family worried about opening
their next medical bill? Why not rip all medical bills and create
a single-payer health security system? Send every high school
graduate to college as long as they can learn to mapquest
their way there! Build the next generation of pyramids with clear
publicly accountable front windows! There are so many jobs waiting
for those who can help build a solar energy cell or write a song
to heal a deeply troubled nation. Let's tickle the bottom of
the economy's feet and watch the electricity rise upward.

October 2008

## Also from Narcissus Press

*Tumbalalaika: a collection of poems* by Diana Ayton-Shenker
Vivid imagery and evocative language depict themes of contemporary
women's identity, Jewish experience, the intimacy of marriage and
motherhood, the pursuit of personal and global freedom through law,
language, and love.

*The Wake-Up Blast: a collection of poems* by Hall Gardner
*The Wake-Up Blast* captures over three decades of poetic protest and
dissent, reflected through the lens of personal experiences and encounters
throughout the world, and explores a wide range of explosive social and
political themes. In interweaving the personal, the social and the political,
Hall Gardner's poetry captivates readers through rallying cries against
fear and violence in a *counter-visionary* quest to transcend the present
global crisis and to achieve mutual understanding among conflicting
peoples and states-through engaged dialogue and the medium of poetry.

www.narcissuspublications.com

**Narcissus Press** is a new literary and visual art publishing enterprise,
specializing in poetry and illustrated literary works. Addressing socio-
political issues through the lens of personal experience and creative
expression, Narcissus showcases emerging and underexposed writers
and artists from Paris, New York City, and upstate New York.

Eliot Katz photo by Vivian Demuth

## About Eliot Katz

Eliot Katz is the author of five previous books of poetry: *When the Skyline Crumbles: Poems for the Bush Years* (Cosmological Knot Press, 2007); *View from the Big Woods: Poems from North America's Skull* (Cosmological Knot Press, 2007); *Unlocking the Exits* (Coffee House Press, 1999); *Les voleurs au travail (Thieves at Work)* (Paris: Messidor Press, 1992, in French translation) and *Space and Other Poems for Love, Laughs, and Social Transformation* (Northern Lights, 1990). He is a coeditor of *Poems for the Nation* (Seven Stories Press, 2000), a collection of contemporary political poems compiled by the late poet Allen Ginsberg. A cofounder and former coeditor of *Long Shot* literary journal, Katz guest-edited *Long Shot's* final issue, a "Beat Bush issue" released in Spring 2004. His essay, "Radical Eyes," is included in the prose collection, *The Poem That Changed America: "Howl" Fifty Years Later.* He is coeditor of a bilingual anthology published in France in 1997, entitled *Changing America: Contemporary U.S. Poems of Protest, 1980-1995.* Called "another classic New Jersey bard" by Allen Ginsberg, Katz worked for many years as a housing advocate for Central New Jersey homeless families. He currently lives in New York City and serves as poetry editor of the online politics quarterly, *Logos: A Journal of Modern Society and Culture.*

You can find his work online at:

www.poetspath.com/exhibits/eliotkatz

William T. Ayton photo by Phil Zemke

## About William T. Ayton

William T. Ayton was born in the north of England, and studied art at Edinburgh College of Art, after showing an early apttude for drawing and painting. Exhibited and published in Europe, Canada, the USA & Israel, his work deals with the human condition, politics & mythology. Seminal pieces include the internationally acclaimed series of paintings depicting The Universal Declaration of Human Rights (U.D.H.R.), a four-wall painted installation called *The War Room*, and a series of painted triptychs on the Holocaust. He has lived in England, Scotland, Spain, France & the USA. He now resides in upstate New York with his wife and partner, Diana Ayton-Shenker, & their 3 children.

You can find his work online at:

>    www.ayton.net
>    www.warroomproject.org
>    www.udhrart.org